What happened to Fr Seán Fagan?

A heartbreaking read! Makes one wonder whether there is any future for a Church governance system that has invested so little internal reflection on the human right to freedom of conscience, opinion and belief and absolutely nothing on due process, justice, truth and the dignity of the human person. Unless conscripted at Baptism noone with a shred of decency could seriously consider joining the Catholic Church until such a dysfunctional system is reformed. There is no visible sign of any such reform being underway. In fact the Church under Francis has deliberately and almost unremarked, slipped backwards in its relationship with UN human rights treaties monitoring bodies. Stories like Seán's deserve to be told and to instruct as this does!

MARY MCALEESE, PRESIDENT OF IRELAND 1997-2011

What happened

to

Fr Seán Fagan?

ANGELA HANLEY

columba
BOOKS

First published in 2019 by

 **columba**BOOKS

23 Merrion Square
Dublin 2, Ireland
www.columbabooks.com

ISBN: 978-1-78218-364-8

Set in Freight Text Pro 10.5/14
Cover and book design by Alba Esteban | Columba Books
Printed by Scandbook, Sweden

In memory of Seán O'Boyle

The Good

The good are vulnerable
As any bird in flight,
They do not think of safety,
Are blind to possible extinction
And when most vulnerable
Are most themselves...
The good incline to praise,
To have the knack of seeing that
The best is not destroyed
Although forever threatened.
The good go naked in all weathers,
And by their nakedness rebuke
The small protective sanities
That hide men from themselves.
The good are difficult to see
Though open, rare, destructible;
Always, they retain a kind of youth,
The vulnerable grace
Of any bird in flight,
Content to be itself,
Accomplished master and potential victim,
Accepting what the earth or sky intends.
I think that I know one or two
Among my friends.

– Brendan Kennelly

CONTENTS

Acknowledgemements — 11

Preface — 13

Introduction — 17

Chapter One: *Growing up* — 21

Chapter Two: *Prophetic theologian* — 45

Chapter Three: *The Universe story* — 59

Chapter Four: *Two (three) books* — 69

Chapter Five: *Accusations* — 81

Chapter Six: *Punishment* — 99

Chapter Seven: *Endgame* — 111

Chapter Eight: *Confrontation* — 125

Chapter Nine: *Things to think about* — 135

Chapter Ten: *Silenced* — 147

Chapter Eleven: *Seán Fagan - Marist priest* — 169

Select Bibliography — 187

References — 201

Acknowledgemements

Most of the research material for this book was given to me by Seán Fagan over the years of our friendship. This was given to me just for my own information at first, then as time passed, it was given for archival purposes with the view to publication.

Material referring to Seán's secondary school days was taken from information he supplied for the necrology of Br Edmund Leonardi Carew (1904-1994) compiled in 1997 by Br Seán O hAnnagáin.

Fr Timothy Radcliffe OP and Mary O'Callaghan gave permission to use their email correspondence about Seán's mistaken 'reprieve'. Br Brendan Geary SM also gave permission to use the content of my discussion with him.

Sr Gabrielle Fox CSsR was especially helpful on religious obedience, offering the most coherent understanding of this counsel.

Brendan Kennelly readily gave permission for the use of his poem *The Good*.

I found the Marist website www.acertainway.org especially helpful for a broad understanding of Marist spirituality which demonstrated how fully Seán Fagan lived his Marist life. The website www.bishop-accountability.org is a very useful resource on the important matter of the behaviour of bishops towards clerical sexual abusers of children.

Thank you to Helen O'Grady and Linda O'Halloran who were attentive readers of earlier drafts of this work.

I would like to thank Maura Morgan and Frankie Kelly for insights into their grandmother's life, which helped me to see the kind and gentle woman more clearly.

As always, Philip Gleeson OP, Librarian in St. Mary's Priory, Tallaght was especially helpful. Alpha Connelly gave generously of her time and expertise to give me insight into human rights law.

I would like to thank Fr Turlough Baxter and Fr Bernard Treacy OP for invaluable assistance in locating some final bibliographical details that had proven elusive.

Special gratitude to my husband Gearoid who retired (early) last year and took over most of the domestic duties. This gave me the most precious gift a writer could have: time.

Preface

Fr Seán Fagan heard many confessions that distressed him by their evidence of how badly many of his penitents had been affected by the sin-obsessed teaching and preaching common at the time. So much of the joy of forgiveness had been lost, and the salvation-tactics of many priests and teachers seemed to rest on the conviction that people could be scared into heaven by fear of hell.

I knew him first as a colleague teaching moral theology in the Milltown Institute. I remember him as a quiet academic, full of good sense often spiced with humour. Seán was a gifted moral theologian who saw that his pastoral experience was revealing problems that were calling out for sane theological examination. His books were very popular and, in the post-Vatican II Church, gave many Catholics a fresh perspective on Christian life, together with relief from the agonising scruples, especially about sex, which were all too common at that time. In short, he wrote the sort of book that offends those who prefer a dark and rule-driven response to moral challenge and its failures.

In the Sermon on the Mount, Jesus reminds us that 'a good tree cannot bear bad fruit, nor can a bad tree bear good fruit' (Matt.7:18). In the light of these words, when one considers the deeds of the Vatican's Congregation for the Doctrine of the Faith (CDF), one may draw some disturbing conclusions about the Congregation itself. What happened to Seán Fagan, and to others like him, is a warning about what can occur when ecclesiastical bureaucrats lose sight of the Gospel and persecute members of their own church for having pastoral and theological ideas that are happily different from their own.

The CDF is the most senior department in the Vatican curia, and the most in need of reform. Even by the standards of an outdated theology, it makes scandalously unjust use of the power that a long history of papal authority in the church has left virtually unchallenged. It speaks threateningly about 'the teaching of the church' which it identifies with its own attitudes.

Seán Fagan was the human face of what high-powered traditionalism can do to men and women of good faith and good pastoral practice. This book will be a lasting reminder of what is usually discussed in purely ideological and abstract terms. The CDF would be happy to keep it abstract and shot through with intimidating power. When we are seeking to understand traditionalism, especially as practised by those with institutional power, it is important not to restrict oneself to semantics, but always to keep in mind its human consequences which relate it directly to the Gospel.

Seán was initially 'silenced', i.e. forbidden to write or communicate in any way with the public. He was threatened with dismissal from his order if he made known anything about what the CDF had done to him. He unselfishly submitted to this because of what excommunication would have meant to his family.

Why this traditionalist flight from transparency in a context which demands it? The Gospel was given with the instruction that it should be announced to the whole world in all its glory and, to use Pauline language, all its scandal. There was nothing secret about it. Its very transparency was, and remains, an essential element in its proclamation to the world. When, in the early 4th Century, the Emperor Constantine ended the persecution of the Christian Church and established it as part of the machinery of imperial government, the way was open to its development as a political body and thus to the sort of corruption associated with power.

Seán was an elderly man, already crippled by painful arthritis among other illnesses. The distress brought about by his treatment at the hands of the CDF was cruel, both physically and mentally. As a priest and religious, his membership of the church was at the very centre of his life. He served the Church to the best of his ability, and the authorities of his church turned on him with savage indifference to his standing in the community and the esteem of his colleagues, to say nothing about his health. Every move made against him professionally was also a move against him personally and was intended to obliterate the memory of a fine theologian, a pastoral priest and member of a religious order. Fortunately, his good friend, Angela Hanley, has agreed to take over Seán's papers so that the story of his treatment by the authorities of his church may be known. Posterity will thank her for her solicitude and skill.

Gabriel Daly OSA

Introduction

This is not strictly a biography, but it tells the story of one man. This is not a work of theology, but gives insight into the mind and heart of one theologian. This is not hagiography for that would insult the man who was all too aware of human frailty. This is a story, a true story, of how one man tried to help the weak, the vulnerable, the heartsore, the burdened and the broken. He did not stand above them but beside them, giving witness to the boundless mercy of God, helping them to understand that they were of equal value to any other person around them. This man is Seán Fagan, SM, a Marist priest who, despite a lifetime of service, suffered at the hands of the Church to which he devoted his whole adult life. That is the story of this book.

Seán did not court fame or publicity, but his charismatic nature and his sound common sense made him well-known. He was often invited to speak at events and to give talks. If he was asked to participate in a radio or television programme, he did. But he never angled for opportunities to be in front of the camera. He had deep respect for journalists and the media generally, though he really disliked sensationalism.

Seán was a humble man in many ways, but very confident in his abilities as a leader, teacher and theologian. He never sought to keep power or position for himself, but constantly encouraged others to believe in themselves and was collegial in his outlook. He had a good sense of humour and a fund of, what he readily admitted were, 'corny stories'. He was a perfectionist, always completing a task to the best of his ability, but tolerant of the failings of others, except of those who should know better – for Seán, this usually meant priests and religious, especially in leadership. He held them to a higher standard.

Seán was an enabler in the most benign and positive meaning of the word. He constantly encouraged and affirmed others, enabling confidence in word and deed. Like any true teacher, his greatest joy was to see a student bloom and grow to independence of thought. He trusted readily and was prepared to accept the outcome of that trust if it proved unjustified. One of his many ready maxims was: "if you are going to trust people, you trust them". He made friends easily and kept them for whatever their natural length. In some cases, it was several years, in others, it was a lifetime.

I came to know Seán in early 1998 having written to thank him for his book *Does Morality Change?*. I had never done anything like that before, but the book made quite an impression on me. I was tired of a Church that really had no respect for women at a fundamental level as people equally formed in the image and likeness of God. At the time I was making my own spiritual preparation for leaving the Church, and in some ways writing to Seán was to be my last action and would allow me to leave on a positive note. Seán responded to my letter with remarkable promptness – within three days, and that was having received the letter via the publisher. As I was to discover later, this efficiency was Seán's *modus operandi*. If there was a job to be done – he just did it.

In his reply, he included copies of articles he thought might interest me. As a courtesy to his kindness in responding, I read and commented upon the articles in my reply, thinking that would be the end of it. But Seán responded again, with even more articles (none his own). This weekly correspondence went on for 18 months. In late 1999 we met for the first time. Following that, we used to meet up two or three times a year as well as writing on a weekly basis – Seán sending me articles, I commenting on them – until 2005. By then, email had taken over along with chats by telephone twice a week.

Because of Seán I stayed part of the Church. I did not feel any more connected to it, but his influence allowed me to stay within and be challenging in the matters I felt strongly about. Before I ever had a chance to study theology, Seán's mentoring had a powerful impact on my thinking. This gave me a tremendous advantage when I eventually got the opportunity to study theology. I already had the vocabulary and the confidence to critically assess and challenge what I was studying. Seán also encouraged me to write on Church-related matters for various religious publications. He never tried to influence anything I had to say, suggesting only that I use my skills to say it publicly.

He was deeply wounded by what happened to him at the hands of the Church he so dearly loved, and which he served so faithfully for 70 years, from when he entered the religious life in 1945 to his death in 2016. The Vatican's doctrinal watchdog, the Congregation for the Doctrine of the Faith (CDF) forced Seán to act against his conscience, that "most secret core, and sanctuary" (according to Vatican II) and extracted a promise of silence from him under duress. To see this story in context, it is necessary to see the person first. What happened to Seán can only be seen in its fullest impact when we get to know the man.

It is a shameful story among so many shameful stories, and as such needs to be recorded. This was Seán's own wish. He wanted his story told after his death. In a short letter to me dated 15 June, 2010 he said: "...you know my decision to keep quiet for the rest of my days, in order to protect my family and friends from the pain and shame of seeing me deprived of priesthood for the remainder of my life. But for the health of our beloved Church it would be good if you found an opportunity... to spill the beans in public on what really went on, to shame our sinful church in the hope that it might prevent further repetitions." To facilitate this, Seán provided me with a dossier of information, which included letters, Vatican documents, emails and other material relevant to his case. Items from this collection will be referenced in the text (*SF Dossier*) together with their access references. I also have an extensive collection of letters resulting from my own personal correspondence with him. These are referenced (PC, date) in the text.

I am both honoured and humbled that Seán left me this task of telling his story. It is no small thing to carry out a person's dying wish – it is both burden and gift. I have carried the burden over the year it has taken to write this book and the previous two years thinking how I might tackle the job. I hope I have been equal to the task and have justified Seán's confidence and trust in me – that is the gift.

CHAPTER ONE

Growing up

Seán Fagan, Marist priest, moral theologian, comforter of the afflicted, afflicter of the comfortable, man of grace, mentor and friend, died quietly not long after sunrise on 15th July, 2016 aged 89. Given the story of his later years, it seemed profoundly fitting that he should come from darkness into light just before he let go of his earthly life.

Over that long life as a dedicated priest and theologian, Seán inhabited completely the description of the Dominican theologian, Marie-Dominique Chenu, who said: "The theologian, unlike the philosopher, works on history. His 'givens' are neither the nature of things nor their eternal forms, but events... And events are always tied to time... This, not the abstraction of the philosopher, is the *real* world." Seán was utterly grounded in the real world and spent a lifetime embodying the gospel he so fervently believed in. There was never discontinuity between his words and actions. He lived his faith, and it was a luminous faith. His God was the prodigal father and mother, boundless in compassion and love. His Church was the mustard tree that had room for everyone to find shelter. As Fr Declan Marmion said in his homily at Seán's funeral Mass: "His vision... was a Church of mercy and compassion, whose first word to people was one of affirmation not condemnation." Though all who came in contact with him felt the power and light of his faith, those who should have valued him for his evangelical witness, his joy in the gospel, made a torment of his final years. It was nothing less that the perpetration of spiritual abuse on an aging and increasingly infirm man.

Though highly intelligent, Seán, in so many ways, was a very simple man. He lived simply within his Marist family. He dressed simply, to the point where a family member or friend had, at times, to intervene and bring him to buy new clothes. He thought excessive interest in clothing was an unbecoming vanity in a priest. He had few personal possessions and those he had were often small gifts of both gratitude and friendship he received from others. He owned a laptop and a modest library of theology books, both of which were extensively used in his ministry of teaching and pastoral care. This simplicity was part of his faith-life and true to his Marist charism that included his vow of poverty. What he needed, the Society provided. If he didn't need it, he shouldn't have it – it was as clear and simple as that. Seán was very critical of clerics who were attached to material goods and trappings of office.

Seán was born on 10th June, 1927 and grew up in Mullingar, Co. Westmeath, then a small provincial town of some 5,000 inhabitants. His mother was Josephine Keilthy from Athy, Co. Kildare, daughter of Mary (Minnie) Sweeney, a housewife, and Patrick Keilthy, a postman. Patrick was from New Ross, Co. Wexford, and Mary was from Co. Limerick. Regular contact was maintained with the Wexford relatives all through Seán's childhood and into his adult life. Seán's father, Peter was the son of James Fagan, a carter, and Mary Callaghan, a housewife, from Mullingar.

Seán's maternal grandmother died from breast cancer when Josephine was about 14 or 15 years old and her father remarried. She felt the loss of her mother deeply and there was not a close relationship with her step-mother. Josephine got a job in the Presentation Convent in Mullingar and that was where she met Peter Fagan. Peter was ten years her senior and after getting to know her while meeting her on his postal rounds, he asked the nuns for permission to date her. This was allowed, and in time they married in the cathedral of Christ the King, Mullingar on 9th June

1926, when Josephine was 18 years old, quite innocent in many respects, and Peter was 28.

The newly-weds settled in Clonmore, Mullingar and between 1927 and 1938, Josephine and Peter had seven children: Seán (baptised John), Patrick, Maura, Kathleen, Teresa, Peter Jr., and Josephine. By Sean's own account, and stories told to her grandchildren by Josephine, Peter Fagan was a very loving husband. He expected the children, once they were old enough, to help their mother with heavy tasks, such as bringing water from the pump or bringing in fuel for the fire. He was quite strict about this, and was very cross with them if they did not do as they were told and left their mother to carry water or coal. Josephine was a dedicated and thrifty housewife. She took pride in her home. Both she and Peter had green fingers and shared a love of gardening. They sowed vegetables and fruit, which provided for jam-making. From Seán's own recollection and that of his nieces and nephews, his mother was an excellent cook and friends of the Fagan children were regular beneficiaries of her treats. She also excelled in knitting and sewing and made all the children's clothes for them. She was utterly devoted to her husband and children. Josephine, for all her innocent ways, had a profound sense of what was right and true. As one grandson says: "She had her priorities in order." She was very firm about never "carrying scandal". She was a woman of deep faith and it informed her life. There was daily prayer, including the rosary. And no doubt this had an effect on her children. Seán certainly attributed his early faith formation to his mother.

In the grim economic circumstances of Ireland in the 1930s and 1940s, Seán led a largely uneventful life in this loving and secure family until he was 15 years old. Until then, the biggest event in his life was being hospitalised for a bout of scarlet fever around Christmastime when he was about six or seven. This was before the power of antibiotics was properly incorporated into medical treatment and when scarlet fever was a potentially fatal disease. He had no visitors due to the danger of spreading the infection. He remembered being lifted up to the window on Christmas morning and seeing his mother below waving up at him. This exception was no small thing back then, and he was told not to tell anyone. This little act of kindness by the nurse brought particular joy to both mother and son during a difficult separation.

Tragedy

Disaster truly struck on Thursday 4th February, 1943 when Seán's father was killed in a traffic accident. Peter Fagan was on his usual postal round at Valley Cottages, Patrick Street when he was struck by an army lorry that had gone out of control on its way into Mullingar. Peter was critically injured with severe head trauma and though he received swift medical attention, he died in the ambulance on the way to hospital. Three soldiers were also seriously injured in the accident and were detained in hospital. A report in the local weekly paper, *The Westmeath Examiner,* on 6th February said "the tragedy cast a gloom over Mullingar and there is heartfelt sympathy with his widow and seven children". Seán was given the news of his father's death on the way to school. A small group of men who saw what happened met Seán on his way back for the afternoon classes and gave him the shocking news without any preparation, telling him that his father was probably dead.

Following this tragedy, Seán's mother was utterly devastated. Josephine told one of her granddaughters many years later that Peter had sheltered and protected her. He had made all the decisions. Now she found herself in her mid-30s without her husband, on whom she depended utterly, as well as having seven children, ranging in age from 15 down to five, to look after. She was almost overwhelmed with grief. She told her granddaughter that one day she left the children with her very good friend and neighbour, Nelly, and walked out into the countryside, climbed into a field, lay down and begged God to take her. After some hours, she realised that her prayer was not going to be answered, and got up and went home to her children.

In the weeks and months afterwards, Josephine most likely suffered severe depression resulting from grief. There were many days she was not able to get out of bed. Even though the neighbours were a wonderful support to the family, and helped in whatever ways they could, Seán, as the eldest, took upon himself the mantle of the father (and sometimes mother) figure to his younger siblings, especially to the two youngest children who were aged just five and six. He said he "fought with God" during that time. Dealing with his own grief for the loss of his father and watching his mother prostrate with grief and despondency was a burden he felt he did not deserve. Yet he cycled to 8 o'clock Mass every morning before going to school.

Eventually, Josephine managed to deal with the worst symptoms of her grief, with great support from neighbours and family, and began to come to terms with her bereavement. There is no doubt that she relied on Seán to help her. She valued his judgement and opinion highly. He, in his turn, was very mature for his age and became someone his mother could lean on. She remarried about 17 years later, but Seán was long gone from home by then, so he did not become particularly close with his stepfather. However, he remained close to his mother until her death in January 1977.

Self-reliant
This experience of tragedy and its consequences had a profound effect on Seán at the time and later influenced his theology. He found himself continually placing the care of others at the heart of all his theological reflection and discussion. He said that in the monastery during his formation he thanked God for the experience of care of his mother and siblings, because from it he gained a strong sense of responsibility. But even more importantly than that, he believed he

tapped into some maternal instinct and sensitivity that might not otherwise have happened. However, the combination of intelligence and experience that helped Seán towards his sense of responsibility and independence was not considered a virtue by some. He found out some years later, when he was working for the Marist General House in Rome after his ordination, that in his file were the words *solum sufficere assuescat*, meaning "he is accustomed to being self-sufficient" (I hope I remember the phrase correctly). He said that this comment was not intended as a compliment. It implied an independence of spirit that was rather frowned upon in a young priest.

Something of this self-sufficiency and the confidence it fostered was already present in Seán from a young age. It meant that he was capable of travelling alone to London to stay with relatives for Christmas 1938. He told me he even brought a turkey with him – a gift from the Mullingar Fagans. He travelled from Mullingar to Broadstone Station, Dublin by himself. There he was met by his Uncle Owen who brought him to his home in Harold's Cross to stay the night. The following day Seán was accompanied to the mailboat by his uncle. As his uncle was making arrangements with the ticket collector to keep an eye on Seán, a friend of Owen's saw them and volunteered, with his two daughters, to look after Seán on the journey. Owen's friend was travelling to Rugby, which was the last stop before Euston and took good care of Seán, buying him a meal on the train from Holyhead. But it was no small feat at age 11 ½ to set out to travel on his own and look after the turkey. When Seán arrived in London he was met by his Uncle Pat, with whose family he was staying in Kennington. He set off on his return journey to Ireland on 2nd January, 1939. As there is no mention in his diary of meeting anybody, I think it is safe to assume he made the return journey from London to Dun Laoghaire on his own. He was met again by his Uncle Owen who gave him a few days holiday in Dublin before setting him on the train, by himself, back to Mullingar.

Seán thoroughly enjoyed his Christmas in London. On Christmas morning there was "an air-gun, a box of crackers, a new penny, a new sixpence and a new shilling in a pillow-case addressed to me". He was delighted with his air-gun and, when he came home, he became quite a sharp-shooter until the day he left a lead pellet in his brother's backside. He claimed it was an accident. His father was extremely angry, thinking of the damage it could have done, so he took the gun and broke it beyond use or repair. Not one for spite, but very angry at losing a treasured possession in this way, Seán drew cartoons of his father, with the face of an orang-utan, smashing the rifle. His father, feeling sorry for Seán, later promised him a bike for school, and peace was restored.

Before he left home on his Christmas adventure, Seán was given a copybook to keep a diary of his journey. Even though he kept it faithfully for the duration of his visit, it did not instil in him any lasting desire for daily journaling. He began the diary on the day he left Mullingar on 16th December, 1938 and finished on the day he left London to come home on 2nd January, 1939. Job done! He did not record anything of his few extra days in Dublin, nor did he mention the turkey on the journey over. Though a deep-thinking man, he wasn't one for introspection. Unlike many priests and religious, Seán did not keep a personal diary. "I toyed with the idea, but personally I'm not attracted to it. Of course, I check on my interior life and try to focus on what is happening and where I'm going, but somehow I feel that I could put the time needed for journal-writing to better use" (PC 03.03.01). There was also the reality that anything Seán had to say, he was prepared to say in public, either through writing, broadcasting, or personal correspondence. There was not a private Seán and a public Seán.

School

Seán's schooldays were uneventful and mostly happy. That he was a very bright student surely helped his easy passage through primary and secondary school. He received his secondary education in the local Christian Brothers school, Coláiste Mhuire, and had much praise for the Brothers who taught him. He particularly admired Br Edmund Leonardi Carew [aka 'E.L.'] who came to Mullingar from Synge St in 1943, serving both as community superior and as school principal. Br Carew was a talented but austere man. However, the young Seán Fagan saw the worth of this dedicated teacher. He said that Br Carew '...was a brilliant teacher, totally dedicated to education, but never in a narrow sense. Every so often he would say something that revealed the deeper spiritual levels of his personality. I remember, even as a teenager, feeling so sorry that hardly anybody in the class would pick up on what he was driving at, or even notice the depths that we occasionally had glimpses of."

E.L. Carew taught Seán higher-level Latin and Maths. And no doubt Br Carew was delighted to have a student of Seán's calibre. As Seán noted, "When he found a student who understood what he was at, and who picked up quickly what he taught, he literally glowed with genuine happiness. It was my great pleasure to see him come alive in this way, and it stimulated me to give of my best." Carew's inspirational teaching gave Seán a lifelong love of Latin. This stood him in good stead when studying in Rome where, as was the norm for clerical students, he did all his studies through Latin. In the summer of 1949, after two years' study in Rome, Seán wrote to thank Br Carew for his teaching, especially of Latin, which served Seán so well in his studies. E.L. replied with gratitude and rather trenchant remarks about being obliged to teach all subjects through the medium of Irish and the poor receptiveness of the lads in Coláiste Mhuire to education! It is interesting to note that although Seán became a polyglot and loved languages, he had no interest whatsoever in maintaining any fluency in the Irish language. He had a strong dislike of the perceived connection between Irish nationalism and the Irish language; any kind of tribalism was anathema to him. He loved language for its own sake, for communication and without political baggage. And who knows, perhaps E.L. Carew's distaste for the imposition of the Irish language across the whole curriculum may have influenced Seán. Or maybe they were more alike than Seán realised. In Sean O hAnnagáin's necrology of E.L. he leaves the last word to E.L.'s niece, who knew him well:

> If I were to summarise his character, I would say that he was very unassuming, with no great interest in material things, determined, single-minded, caring and with great interest in his family. He seemed to have no time for rules and regulations that made no sense to him. He was a man of prayer.

As succinct a description of Seán Fagan that anyone is likely to get.

The ability of Seán to perceive and profit from the ability and experience of others served him well later in his pastoral ministry. As bright as he was, and as knowledgeable as he was, he never assumed he knew it all. He was always willing to learn. He even taught himself art as a teenager and got 1st place in Ireland in his Leaving Certificate exam. A close friend at the time also was self-taught, and he came second. Granted, in the 1940s, few people from Seán's socio-economic background got to secondary school, even fewer reached Leaving Certificate and, one imagines, even fewer again took art as a subject. However, it offers insight into the auto-didact he was. Challenges were simply hills to be climbed, so that the view from the summit could be appreciated.

Not sporty

Seán wasn't particularly sporty but all his life he loved swimming, not competitively, just for the sheer pleasure of it. It became a meditative experience for him as he grew older, because he loved simply to float in the water. This could be at midnight in the sea at Kerry looking up at the stars, or in the Mediterranean during holiday time, whenever he was based in Rome. "In the Mediterranean I can almost sleep in the water, buoyed up in a natural all-embracing element. I often make a present participle of the noun 'faith' and think of so much of my faith-life as 'faithing,' being embraced, lifted up and carried (like an infant in the womb) in so very-natural element of God's ever present and infinite love." (PC, 30.11.99)

Oddly, given his peace-loving temperament, he did join the local boxing club in Mullingar. However, he preferred the technical skill of boxing and to win on points than any desire to thump his opponent into submission. His lack of sporting interest was a cause of much frustration late in life, when his confrères would rather talk about rugby or golf and Seán wanted to discuss matters of current affairs, opinion columns (he was a fan of Fintan O'Toole, especially) or matters theological or spiritual. And one can imagine they were likely equally frustrated by Seán's preference for theology and spirituality over even occasional sport. At times, this disparity of interests left him feeling isolated within his community, but that was just one more burden to be carried.

Seán was never nostalgic about his childhood or the past. His background was humble, but he neither boasted of, nor hid, the fact. He marked that which was good and affirming; he was philosophical about that which was tough or challenging. He saw opportunities for growth and learning in all experiences. He had good relationships with both his parents, but felt a particular closeness to his mother. He always believed that his family grounding was the foundation on which he built his later life, but there was no rose-tinted, romanticised, polished-up version. It was what it was – simple, plain, unremarkable, ordinary, decent.

Vocation

Like many idealistic secondary school leavers of the time, Seán had the noble intentions of wanting to do something worthwhile with his life in the service of others. Thoughts of religious life were among the first to be considered. This is hardly surprising given his immersion in the Catholic culture of the time – family rosary, daily Mass, May devotions, Blessed Sacrament processions, various novenas, sodalities and the rote question-and-answer of childhood catechesis. He bought religious books with his very limited pocket money: lives of the saints, *The Imitation of Christ* by Thomas a Kempis, *Introduction to the Devout Life* by Francis de Sales. Staple fare for anyone inclined towards the religious at the time. One quite influential book at the time was Jean-Pierre de Caussade's *Abandonment to Divine Providence*. In this book Seán discovered the idea of "the sacrament of the present moment". This concept affected him profoundly. Perhaps the experience of his father's tragic death when Seán was only 15 years old helped him to be open to the idea. This lodged within him and remained an influence throughout his life. Through it he valued friendships, for however long or short in duration, or geographical distance or nearness. He never had any desire to hold onto a connection that had reached its natural end. It was also deeply influential in his spirituality. It was the inspiration for an article he wrote in 1971 called 'It's good to be here' which gives good insight into his spirituality. This was a piece of writing that remained his personal favourite throughout the rest of his life. A close second was 'Sacraments in the spiritual life' published in 1974, but more on both of these later.

Responding to the call to priesthood, Seán never desired to be a diocesan priest – whether or not he could have articulated it at the time, but the idea of community was very important to him. He toyed with the idea of joining the Cistercians and cycled to Mount Melleray Abbey from New Ross, while on holidays, to spend a come-and-see weekend in their monastery. This kind of cycling was nothing new to Seán. In the summers of 1943, 44 and 45, he cycled 110 miles from Mullingar to New Ross for holidays with his maternal family relations. He developed a bit of a teenage 'crush' on one of his cousins during the summer of 1945, but his aunt, the girl's mother, put a very firm and definite stop to it in a strongly worded letter to him after he'd gone home. He was rather taken aback at the vehemence of his aunt's words, but in what became his way to do things, he wrote back with kindness and an apology for upsetting her, which defused the situation.

In thinking about priesthood, Seán was very strongly oriented towards missionary work. He regularly read *The Far East* magazine and this sparked the missionary impulse. He considered working with leper colonies in Africa. However, it was a Marist priest who conducted a school retreat who convinced Seán that his future was with the Society of Mary (Marist Fathers). Seán began a correspondence with the priest after the retreat and maintained it until he entered the congregation. This practice of school visitation was a common recruiting method for the priesthood in Ireland at the time and continued right up to the 1970s at least.

Joining the Society of Mary

Though Seán was awarded a university scholarship on the results of his Leaving Certificate, he did not take it up. The 'uni schol,' as it was colloquially known, was awarded by the local authority (in this case, Westmeath County Council) on the basis of both means and examination results. Instead, immediately on leaving school in 1945, Seán joined the Marist Fathers. After a year in Milltown, Dublin, he spent a year in spiritual studies in Paignton in the south of England. Then in 1947, after his profession as a member of the Marists, he went to continental Europe and spent eight, what he called, "marvellous years" beginning in Rome, living and studying in an international atmosphere. He made his final profession on 12th September, 1950 in Fürstenzell in south-eastern Germany, near the Austrian border, where the Marists have had a presence since the early 20th Century. The sisters of the Presentation Convent in Mullingar were extremely supportive of Seán's vocation. They helped his mother by contributing to the specified clothing that he needed to bring with him when he first entered the Marists as a novice. Seán was ordained a priest on 28th June, 1953 in Rome. His mother was able to travel to attend the occasion and one imagines the Presentation Sisters may have had a hand in that too.

Seán studied four years of philosophy and four years of theology in the *Angelicum*, the Dominican college in Rome. He qualified with a Licentiate in Theology and a Doctorate in Philosophy. On one occasion, when we were discussing education in general and theological education in particular, I asked Seán what the subject of his doctoral dissertation was and he mumbled something. I just managed to catch the words "Aquinas" and "Whitehead". Anyone who knew Seán, knew his appreciation of diction and clear communication, so this mumbling was most uncharacteristic. I asked again, with a request for a bit more volume and clarity. At which Seán actually blushed (something he rarely did) and said more clearly: *"The eternal objects in the philosophy of Aquinas and of Alfred North Whitehead"*. He was embarrassed by the whiff of ivory tower theology it implied. Despite the esoteric title, Seán managed to make it a readable work as I discovered on a visit to the library of the Marist General House when my husband Gearóid and I spent a memorable few days in Rome, with Seán, to celebrate our 25th wedding anniversary in 2005.

A part of Seán's education that he truly appreciated and stood him in good stead over the years were his summer months away from formal study in Rome. Along with fellow-students he spent time in other parts of Italy, France, Spain and Germany. While in Spain, for a short break from 10 weeks teaching, he made a two-day trip to Portugal in 1952, travelling by train, primarily to visit Fatima. He had only $2 as pocket money and existed on coffee and grapes for the visit. Seán's gift for languages was given free rein at this time and he achieved a fluency that allowed him to give retreats and renewal courses for religious in later years. In the years 1987-95, he served as moderator, facilitator and translator to 30 provincial or regional chapters of religious around the world and to 20 international chapters.

This experience is not to be under-estimated in the years from the late 1940s to the early 1960s, a time when Ireland was intellectually, religiously, spiritually, politically as well as geographically insular. In his book, *Ireland 1912-1985, politics and society*, J.J. Lee said:

> *Irish life abounds whether in the senior civil service, in university, administration, or among academics themselves, with people of high, but narrow intelligence. It is impossible not to wonder how much more of their own potential they might have realised if only they had enjoyed exposure to wider intellectual cultures.* (p.615)

According to an interview in *The Sunday Independent* of 16th November, 1975, Seán possessed "a sophistication rare in Irish people and probably gained from his many years abroad in various European countries". He loved this international experience and gained a deep appreciation, which was reinforced in his later travels, for the role of culture in the formation of the person in society. This international influence was also to profoundly affect his theology precisely because of this understanding of cultural conditioning. And the more he interacted with people from around the globe, the more convinced he became about the importance of the effect of cultural conditioning and how it had to be factored into theological discussion.

Altogether, Seán spent 25 years in Rome, though not consecutively. In the first period most of the time was as a student (1947-1955) and later (in between time spent back in Dublin, teaching) he spent variously, a year as private secretary to the Marist superior general, which included the first Synod of Bishops after the Second Vatican Council, a year doing research with two confrères (1967-68);

a year as Superior of the Marist international house of studies, Via Cernaia, Rome (1969-70). In his second period in Rome, Seán spent 12 consecutive years, from 1983 to 1995, in the Marist General House on Via Alessandro Poerio, serving as Secretary General of the Marists for three four-year terms.

Ministry

His ministry and service in Ireland included teaching philosophy, moral theology and some scripture in Mount St Mary's, Milltown, the Marist house of studies, from 1955-60. He served as Superior in Mount St Mary's from 1961-1967, during which time he oversaw a significant building project in the expansion of the house of studies, for which he drew up the plans himself. From 1970-73 he conducted retreats in the Marist Retreat Centre, St Doolagh's Park, Raheny, Dublin, as well as teaching moral theology in the Milltown Institute. He taught in Mount St Mary's, the Milltown Institute and the Mater Dei Institute during 1973-83. Despite his great passion for teaching he still had the common sense to tell students: "Don't let study interfere with your education!" That school or college was not the only place for receiving useful education was something that Seán regularly espoused.

During this time, Seán also gave talks to parishes and groups. He was involved peripherally in the charismatic renewal as a renewal movement in the Church, rather than especially committed to it as a movement in itself. He saw his role as bringing a little common sense to some of the more enthusiastic groups, heavily influenced by emotion rather than spirituality. And of course during all this time, he continued to write articles. In 1999 he moved from the community in Mount St Mary's to the CUS community in Lower Leeson Street, Dublin City. He had no direct role in the secondary school (Catholic University School) run by the Marists, but helped out hearing confessions when required. In the CUS community he served in the Marists' public Church, which had its own dedicated community. He also looked after the smooth running of the women's hostel that the Marists provided on the top floor of their buildings in Leeson Street. Mostly international students found accommodation here. This also involved practical matters such as sorting leaks and blockages. More than once Seán found the wiring from underwire bras clogging pipes in the washing machines and had to put up a notice asking the women to remove all such dangers before loading machines with clothes! During this time, he continued with adult education in the Milltown Institute, right up to the end of 2007, which was a source of great satisfaction and fulfilment. He thrived on the enthusiasm of the student who was learning from desire rather than obligation. He was very sad when he was informed that his services were no longer required in Milltown, because they were changing the format of their adult education programme in the Institute.

In his first period working in Rome, Seán bought a Moto Guzzi 125cc motorcycle to get around the city. He loved that motorbike! He had it for 20 years, bringing it back to Dublin when he was moved back to Ireland from Rome. It was a source of particular annoyance to him that a confrère who was given the motorbike some years later, when Seán no longer needed it, managed to wreck it beyond use. During his first period in Rome, he did the Rome-Dublin journey twice, once in 1969 and once in 1970 on the Moto Guzzi. It meant travelling 13 hours a day for three days, plus another half-day's travelling to complete the journey. Of course, he then undertook the return journey after the summer break. But the journey wasn't just a means to an end, of getting from departure to destination. The journey itself was part of the enjoyment. In many ways that reflected the man – though he was task-oriented, he also took time to look at, and appreciate, the world around him.

There were many people in Ireland who perceived his second period away as a deliberate dislocation to Rome in order to remove Seán from the Irish Church. By 1983, he had appeared many times on

TV, including *The Late Late Show,* hosted by Gay Byrne, along with other religious programmes. He had contributed to radio and had written regularly to the *Letters to the Editor* of newspapers as well as contributing occasional articles when requested. He contributed regularly to religious periodicals. He was also involved in adult education.

When Seán spoke, people listened. Quite apart from the qualities of his speaking voice, which was soft and gentle though perfectly enunciated and clear, the content of what he had to say was what captured the imagination of many. I asked Seán about this perception of his move to Rome. Was it his opinion that he was moved to get this 'turbulent priest' out of circulation? He truly did not believe this was so. At the time there were internal administrative problems within the Marist Generalate, and a General Secretary was required at rather short notice. Seán was chosen for the job by the governing body. But there remained the perception among many that Seán had been strategically moved. A letter writer to *The Irish Times,* Carmel Lavelle, was delighted when Seán made an appearance, sometime after his return in December 1995, in the Letters page of the same paper. It's worth reproducing the full text:

> Sir, - My heart leapt with joy when I saw the name of Father Seán Fagan SM at the bottom of a letter to *The Irish Times.* I still remember with excitement his lectures given in Dun Laoghaire at a time when the late Father Chris Mangan instituted a mini-renaissance in Christianity in that parish (a movement that quickly smothered when that prophetic priest retired).
>
> When Father Fagan was effectively silenced by being transferred to Rome, I never expected to hear his voice, which spoke in the true spirit of Vatican II, again. May we hear more from Father Fagan, a man who speaks from deep conviction and one whose pedigree is untainted, either with ambition or a desire for popularity. - Yours, etc.

Apart from his theological expertise, Seán was also a very able and gifted administrator. He was a highly organised person and very efficient. He was a perfectionist – if any job was worth doing, it was worth doing right. He readily embraced new technology as it emerged, and used it to great effect in his work. He had almost a holy reverence for the invention of the laptop. This was part of the simplicity of the man – his awe and wonder at the minds that conceived the technology and then who brought it into being. A computer wasn't just a tool – it was a sign of the wondrous creativity of the human mind.

During his three four-year terms as Secretary General to the Society of Mary, Seán was the Procurator to the Holy See, which is the nominated person to deal with the Vatican departments on behalf of the Marist Fathers. He also was responsible for a number of Councils of the Society in Quebec, Madrid and Suva (Fiji), as well as general chapters of the Society in 1985 and 1993. General chapters are a gathering of regional delegates of a religious order or congregation. In the case of an international congregation such as the Marist Fathers, this would be a gathering from around the world. During this time, Seán also translated the Constitutions of the Society of Mary from Latin into English.

On top of this, Seán served as treasurer and an executive committee member of SEDOS, a progressive and active association of 86 religious congregations [in 1995] involved in global mission. It represented over a quarter of a million religious around the world at that time. He also facilitated most of its seminars.

Seán's 'family'

Seán had a very broad definition of family. He had a rhyme that he had picked up along the way and liked to drop into a conversation: "There is a destiny that makes us brothers and sisters; none go their way alone; all that we send into the lives of others comes back into our own." (*A Creed*, Edwin Markham) He said that this was his own experience over and over again. His understanding of relationships was grounded in his understanding of God – we see God in other people. The deeper our encounter with God, the deeper our relationships with others.

He loved his family of origin. When his siblings married and had children, he delighted in the wonderment of his nieces and nephews as they grew into the world. He was immensely proud of their achievements. He had a particular facility with crying babies and seemed to be able to calm them easily! He also could get toddlers and small children to stand and balance in one of his hands – he used this to demonstrate the trust of a small child. He held their two feet tight in one of his hands and they stood up straight.

He loved his Marist family. That is not to say he thought everything was perfect about it, he didn't and he certainly struggled in his later years. But he was deeply rooted in the Marist charism "to proclaim the gospel to the people of our time, ever conscious of the mystery of Mary in the Church" and he was loyal to the Irish Congregation of the Society of Mary. After spending the second extended period in the General House in Rome (1983-1995), the Italian Province of the Marist Fathers invited Seán to become part of their community before he was due to leave in 1995, but he declined. He loved Italy and it would have suited him perfectly to remain. He used to tell his Italian friends: "sono Romano di cuore," (I am, by heart, a Roman) but in his own eyes he 'belonged' to the Irish Province – it was his family. There were times when he had some regrets about this. Especially from 1997-99 while superior in Mount St Mary's, Milltown. There were obviously personality clashes, resentments on the part of some and the general difficulty of working with people in community. As Seán said: "I am still very much in culture shock, missing the international scene..." and that he felt for some of his confrères, "...I am still a foreigner. It hurts to feel like a stranger in my own home, in Milltown of all places" (*SF Dossier/BK/ SF/JH/98-03(c)*). Yet for all that, Seán still believed he did the right thing in coming back to Ireland. For him, it was a manifestation of his vow of obedience, a freely chosen decision to remain loyal to his Irish Marist family, even if at times it was a struggle for him. One of Seán's deepest difficulties in his later years was his perception of religious communities as little more than institutionalised bachelors who just happened to occupy the same living space. He believed having a vibrant, communal spiritual and prayer life was central to living the religious life. He felt that it was a critical aspect missing from the community to which he returned after his 12 years in Rome. As a friend in whom he confided much, I believe that his sense of being the outsider was never fully resolved in his remaining years in Dublin.

Seán's notion of family extended to all he met and encountered in his ministry. There was the family of friends – with which he was well-endowed – and the family of the students he taught. He found particular joy in teaching adults in the evening programmes of theology in the Milltown Institute. There was the family of the worshipping community – those who gathered to celebrate Eucharist. Seán looked at the world through the lens of creation. Everything is God-given and beautiful, especially people. He enjoyed nothing better, when based in Leeson Street, than to walk through St Stephen's Green. At times he "found it difficult not to let the tears flow at the beauty, wonder and mystery of it all – the profusion of flowers, the great variety of people strolling through, each one so different, each one infinitely precious in God's sight, and the simple incarnations of God's love in the touch of a hand, the care for a little toddler taking first steps in God's creation. For me, all of that is the context for sacraments" (PC 18.03.00). For Seán, we all belong to one another in the family of God, which is not just the Catholic family, nor even the Christian family, but the whole human family.

The 'other' is part of me

This inclusiveness, the appreciation of the 'other,' the understand-ing of cultural conditioning, the God of prodigality and the limit-less capacity of Church to hold all in its embrace, sums up Seán's spirituality. This spirituality, like the rest of his approach to life, was simple. It reflected the kindness and compassion of Jesus as portrayed in the gospels. With that kindness and compassion there was also a steely determination to call to account those in power who mediated a harsh and unforgiving Church. Seán's constant mission was to help people understand the prodigality of God's love – we all matter, we are all loved by God without reference to privilege or status. He told me that there were many times in the past he was on the verge of tears after hearing confessions. In the confessional he witnessed the damage done by the Church to people's sense of self, their poor moral development, the crushing sense of guilt, a flawed understanding of sexuality and the des-perate scruples that many suffered. He called this spiritual abuse. After reading an article by Fr Donal Dorr in *The Furrow* (Oct 2000, pp.523-531) where Dorr, a fellow theologian, identified spiritual abuse as a reality, Seán was inspired to write an article on the subject that was published by *Doctrine & Life* in 2001. He called spiritual abuse "a moral disease that has affected the Church for centuries". He names it as "an abuse of power and authority, and not simply the result of ignorance". In his list of matters he calls spiritual abuse is mandatory clerical celibacy, the refusal to ordain women, the prohibition of 'artificial' contraception and calling LGBTI people intrinsically disordered. He also points out that "murderers, serial rapists and paedophile priests have free access to Holy Communion while committed Catholics who have suffered marital breakdown but now find the grace and intimacy of God in a new relationship are forbidden the sacrament". This, too, he includes in instances of spiritual abuse.

A significant part of the appreciation of the 'other' was Seán's ministry to Catholic gay men in the late 1970s. In an interesting initiative for its time, the President and Vice-President of a praesidium of the Legion of Mary in Dublin decided on an outreach to gay men. At that time, the common meeting places for gay men were public toilets and certain gay-friendly bars. These two men invited a Redemptorist priest Fr Raphael Gallagher, whom they heard speak at a lecture, to assist them. They spent time working in this ministry reaching out to men trying to evangelise and encourage them away from casual sex. Unexpectedly, they also found themselves being evangelised by the gay men in turn. By listening, they began to understand something of the stresses and difficulties of being gay at a time when proper, consenting adult relationships were illegal in both civil law and Church law. Eventually, the time constraints between the work of the gay outreach and the Legion meant the men had to make a choice. They moved away from the Legion and continued their ministry with the men.

Without the structure and oversight of the Legion of Mary, the gay men involved began to open up and discuss what it meant to be gay and Catholic in Ireland. They wanted to have a faith context where they could meet and their sexuality could be openly acknowledged. Facilities were made available in Marianella, the Redemptorist house in Rathgar, Dublin for the group to meet. Fr Raphael realised that they could not advance the cause of the group themselves and so contacted a number of priests he felt would be sympathetic, many of whom were well known. One of these was Fr Seán Fagan. Not only was Seán present at meetings to help guide and discuss, he also spoke privately to individuals by phone and engaged in private correspondence – he could always be relied upon to give efficient, compassionate and focused responses. Many of the men relied upon Seán as a personal guide and support. From about 1980, members of the group saw that some kind of structure would be helpful to its functioning. Seán, given his talent for administration, was an integral part of that conversation. The group formed themselves into an organisation called Reach, which flourished until the 1990s. During that time Seán, whether in Rome or Dublin, was a constant support to the organisation and to individual members.

This kind of apostolate was not unusual for Seán, especially the willingness to carry on a correspondence or receive phone calls from people in emotional or spiritual need or distress. He had "interesting contact" with quite a number of cross-dressers. One person used to write lengthy letters to him a few times a year. The letters could be between 25-30 typed pages of A4 of single-line spacing. This man was "a very devout Catholic" who had his wife's understanding regarding his cross-dressing. The man died in the early 1990s and, afterwards, his wife came to see Seán when visiting Ireland (PC 14.06.00).

Busy though he was, with his own work, or work within whatever Marist community with whom he was living, Seán never resented the demands on his time by people in need. His first instinct was service. He occasionally used Tagore's quote: "I slept and dreamt that life was joy. I awoke and saw that life was service. I acted and behold, service was joy." In this, he lived his Marist charism faithfully.

The communion of saints

Last, but not least, there was the family of the communion of saints. Seán felt a profound connection with all those who have gone before us in faith. He felt this particularly with a close friend, Sr Maura O'Connor, who was one of three blood sisters who were members of the Marist Sisters. Seán met Maura in Rome in the early 1960s when religious sisters took Vatican II very seriously and started their *aggiornmento* (to use the phrase of John XXIII – it means 'updating'). That Seán and Maura would become friends and soul mates, despite their separate lives, for over 40 years is not surprising. In 1998 another Marist sister, then in her mid-80s, told Seán that Maura was "the greatest intellectual of the Province for so many years". And this was at a time when the Anglo-Irish Province had more than 200 sisters. She also said that Maura was an excellent teacher and a "great nun" in the best sense of the word (*Homily*, 18.07.98).

Maura and her family were from Kerry and Seán spent many a happy holiday near Tralee when Maura, her sisters, Sr Paul and Sr Brigid (died, 2013), their sister Peg, and other family members met up during the summer holidays. Sadly, Maura died suddenly in July 1998. One Saturday morning, she felt a little weak and decided to lie down for a while but "the moment didn't pass, the moment was transformed into eternity" (*Homily*, 18.07.98). She was just 70 years old, with much left to offer. Maura had died, but to Seán that was simply moving to a different realm of existence. She was still a real presence to him. "My dear friend Maura has come to my help in so many ways since July last. In fact, even when I don't invoke her or contact her, when things just slot into place for me unexpectedly I can't help feeling her presence" (PC, 07.03.99). Several years later, Seán still spoke of the unseen, but often felt, presence of Sr Maura in his life. For as long as he was able, he travelled to Kerry every July to celebrate Maura's anniversary Mass with her family, which he considered part of his own extended family.

Apart from the immediacy of direct personal contact with people when in conversation, teaching or personal correspondence, Seán's next most useful way to reach out to the wider Church was through writing. He always saw the Church as the people, the assembly, the gathering of the faithful, not the monolithic institution with clerics to the fore. Seán's writings were never about abstract theories, but always about reaching out, educating and helping to lift people's burdens. The immediacy and impact of this can be seen from his moderation of the *Family Matters* page in *The Universe* newspaper. But before we look at this, it is necessary to consider Seán the prophetic theologian because it is this aspect of the man that had the most profound effect on others.

CHAPTER TWO

Prophetic theologian

As a moral theologian, in a pastoral ministry that spanned more than 50 years, Seán Fagan produced two important books, *Has Sin Changed?* and *Does Morality Change?* (see Chapter Four) and a rewrite of *Has Sin Changed?* entitled *What Happened to Sin?*. He wrote in excess of 100 articles, more than 140 book reviews (valuable as mini-tutorials in theology given his knowledge of the comparative literature) and participated in many radio and television broadcasts. Through these mediums he asked questions about, and offered answers to, a wide variety of issues that needed discussion within the Catholic Church.

Prophecy almost inevitably conjures up the misguided notion of clairvoyance or the foretelling of events. But the theologian as prophet is not engaged in such useless activities. She or he is often the voice of the alienated calling authorities to account, challenging them to "face, embrace and engage" with the realities of lives quite unlike their own. The prophets in ancient Israel called either the kings or the religious leaders to account. They were 'a disturber of Israel'. A modern equivalent is the 'disturber of the Vatican,' so also is the person calling on civil government to enact policies to protect the poor, the weak and the vulnerable. They will also challenge corruption where they see it. In ancient times the religious and secular worlds were deeply intertwined, there was no clearly delineated religious and secular sphere. Prophets in antiquity arose from all sections of society, they were not confined to religious leaders and priestly castes. Equally, it is the case today. However, given the hegemony of the Church for the greater part of 2,000 years, the non-clerical prophet was a voice easily ignored. The more notable figures revered tended to be clerics.

The prophetic person

The prophetic person is characterised by a strong personal relationship with God and consequently develops concern for the wider community. Such a person is not only true to the heart of the message of the religious tradition but highly sensitive to the historical moment and the 'signs of the times'. Such a prophetic person is in tune with the political, social, economic and social reality of the society within which she or he functions. "Human history with all its possibilities, challenges and risks is the matrix within which the reign of God takes shape. Its dynamism and novelty can be neither repressed nor ignored, for it mirrors the creativity of God." (*New Dictionary of Theology*, p.783) The prophet is deeply compassionate, profoundly God-centred and utterly devoted to the service of others.

In other words, a prophet is a person who asks the awkward questions of church and of state not just because they are awkward, but because such questions require answers, especially as a response to the 'signs of the times'. The prophets do not just ask the questions, but are also willing to offer some answers, because they are not exercising their gift for themselves. They are at the service of the community. Seán Fagan was such a person. All his writing, including his books, certainly read 'the signs of the times' for the Church itself. And in the sad, sorry tradition of punishing prophets, he too did not escape the attentions of those who would silence his voice.

Seán had been talking sound sense since he started writing. For example, in an article on seminary training more than 50 years ago, he said:

...authority should be explained as service, with emphasis on the obligation to consult, discuss... This kind of training in the seminary would save many a priest the trouble he makes for himself by treating his parishioners as children.

(*The Furrow*, May 1965, pp.267-76)

Long before the wider Church knew the breadth and depth of the scandal of clerical sexual abuse of children and the efforts made by so many bishops to cover it up, he wrote in 1992:

What should our response be to this phenomenon? Very simply: admit, accept, adjust. We must first admit that paedophilia is a reality among priests and religious. ...It is a problem of our society at large, and since religious are members of that society, it is only to be expected that they will reflect their own share of the weaknesses found in the general population. As religious we need to accept this fact, not reject it or rationalise it. ...The matter is too serious for less than full openness.

(*Religious Life Review*, Nov-Dec 1992, pp.317-20).

With all that has come to light since these words were written in 1992 right up to the present day, one cannot but think if Seán's words had been taken seriously at the time, the Catholic Church might not now be crumbling under the weight of its own deceit in what it claimed it did and did not know over the years when people came to priests and bishops with credible claims of sexual abuse.

It is worth noting that Seán's words were written a year before Fr Kevin Hegarty who, as editor of *Intercom*, published an article by Limerick social worker, Philip Mortell, on the impending disaster for the Church because of clerical child sexual abuse. The *Intercom* article was in the form of 20 questions to the bishops on the matter. This was long before the Brendan Smyth exposé and resulted from Mr Mortell's contact with individuals and families as a social worker, and the stories he was being told. *Intercom* is published by Veritas, which, at the time, was owned by the Irish bishops and is directed at diocesan priests. The speed with which Kevin Hegarty was removed from his job and dispatched to a small rural parish in west Mayo was extraordinary. This efficiency of action is thrown into high-relief when compared with the inactions of a number of Irish bishops with regard to clerical sexual abuse of children as shown in the various reports.

Calling leadership to account

Seán remained dogged in calling the Church leadership to account with regard to clerical child sexual abuse. However, another type of abuse reared its ugly head: the abuse of religious sisters by priests in developing countries. In 1994 there was a report submitted to the Vatican by a senior missionary sister in Africa, Sr Maura O'Donoghue, a Medical Missionary of Mary and medical doctor. In her work on AIDS prevention, she started hearing horrendous stories about this type of abuse. In 1998, Sr Marie McDonald, a member of the Missionary Sisters of our Lady of Africa also submitted a report on the abuse of nuns. Her information came from a variety of diocesan congregations and from the Conference of Major Superiors in Africa, so she was confident of its truth. She listed similar situations to Sr O'Donoghue – abuse, rapes, pregnancies, abortions. Nobody in authority wanted to know about this, neither the relevant department in the Vatican, members of which did not act upon the 1994 report, nor the meeting of African bishops who in 1998 received Sr Marie McDonald's report. It took the progressive American Catholic newspaper *National Catholic Reporter* (see ncronline.org) to break the story in 2001. Even at that, the story really did not make the headlines it deserved internationally.

Probably because of his retreat and renewal work with various women's congregations over many years, Seán felt particular empathy for the religious sisters suffering abuse. He called upon the authorities to strip such priests of their "pedestals of power, their priestly status in the community. To complain about losing the huge amounts of money invested in their formation and training is to forget the gospel, to get our priorities wrong." (*Religious Life Review,* May-June 2001, pp.146-156) As always, Seán placed the human over the institution, placed social and spiritual capital over financial capital. Following publication of this article, he received phone calls and letters from Dublin, London, Rome, the United States and Africa, all in gratitude that he spoke out on an issue that had been shrouded in silence and inaction despite the best attempts of two loyal Churchwomen to have it raised in the right quarters.

In October 2001, Sr Maura O'Donoghue met with Seán for a long conversation. She outlined just how big and how difficult a problem the abuse of nuns and sisters is. Seán was deeply impressed with her and her fight for justice in the face of implacable resistance from the Church leadership in Rome and in Africa (PC 10.10.01). As recently as September 2018, there was a well-publicised case of an Indian nun raped by her bishop. Not only was her claim ignored by the nation's bishops, but she was disowned by her own leadership for being courageous enough to bring her assault into the light. The police officer investigating the case has concluded that the accused bishop had raped the nun. As with the history of clerical sexual abuse in Ireland, the reputation of the Church was being put ahead of justice, so despite the fact the bishops had this information from the police, they did nothing to make their brother bishop take responsibility for his actions. The nuns and those supporting their call for justice are branded "enemies of the Church" (*The Tablet,* 29.09.18, pp.10-11). A woman who helped the Indian bishops draw up two important documents on zero tolerance of violence towards women and sexual harassment in the workplace asks: how can the bishops remain neutral on this issue and claim they've no authority to take action against a bishop who clearly has a case to answer? Indeed. That was always Seán's contention: how could those who are charged with the spreading the gospel oversee some of the most awful injustices perpetrated against children and vulnerable adults?

This issue was raised again at the synod on abuse in Rome in February 2019 – time will tell whether or not it will be acted upon. Past attitudes and inaction do not fill one with confidence.

Ecumenism

Seán had a very strong ecumenical conviction. He believed in continual dialogue and sharing, which included knowing you had something to learn from the other person/tradition. When former President Mary McAleese, in a first step towards the bridge-building that was the watchword of her presidency, took Communion in Christ Church Cathedral, Dublin, on 7th December, 1997, Seán was very supportive. Controversy erupted immediately, as might be expected. Among others, Fr James McEvoy, then professor of philosophy in St Patrick's College, Maynooth and Msgr Denis Faul, the prominent Northern Ireland priest and civil rights campaigner, were both very angry about it. The former accused President McAleese of having a "liberal, do-it-yourself, two fingers up to the bishops agenda" while the latter said no Catholic had the right to take Communion in a Protestant church and this applied to "the Pope in Rome and Mary McAleese as much as it does to Paddy and Biddy Murphy".

Never to be found wanting, Seán added his voice to the debate in a letter to *The Irish Times*, published 1st-2nd January, 1998. This letter was taken up with some minor editing both by *The Irish News* and the *Belfast Telegraph*, and published with his permission, as a contribution to the peace process. The letter was obviously circulated in the United States because Seán received some feedback from there also. A Church of Ireland rector in Dublin made

700 copies of the letter and distributed them to his congregation on the following Sunday because, he said: "we have something to learn".

It is worth reproducing the greater part of the letter here:

>...Clerical references to "Church teaching" focus exclusively on words and documents, forgetting that Jesus taught in word and deed - and his deeds were often more powerful and more revealing than his words. History shows that the Church's teaching produced some atrocious documents (now conveniently forgotten), as well as some splendid writings expounding the Christian message. But Church leaders do not seem to realise what they preach by their actions, and actions speak louder than words. Their most effective teaching ought to be the silent sermon of their example.
>
>There is a real scandal in the fact that our President should be attacked for following her maturely formed conscience (a most basic teaching of the Church), but not a word of reprimand was uttered (at least in public) in condemnation of the intemperate, ill-mannered and totally ungospel outbursts of Frs James McEvoy and Denis Faul. The "theology" reflected in their thinking is simply appalling, but of course neither of them is a professional theologian.
>
>With regard to the President's Communion, too many people blame the media for turning it into a scandal, but the media people do their job and clerics must accept the risk of having the spotlight turn on themselves. They need to remember sometimes that the best way to save face is to keep the lower half closed. Rash judgment is a sin, and it is a real scandal to hear clerics attributing unworthy motives to our President in expressing her Christian faith in a profound act of worship. Those who question her theology might reflect

51

that she is more theologically literate than some clerics who have not read a book since ordination.

Some say that she gave a bad example in her disobedience to current canon law, which forbids this kind of inter-communion. But it needs to be remembered that if committed Christians had never disobeyed laws that outlived their original usefulness, the Church would never have outgrown the cultural conditioning of earlier centuries and it would still be defending torture, slavery, and just war, and condemning freedom of conscience and of religion as "madness" (Pius IX, 1864), or as "an erroneous and absurd opinion" (Gregory XVI, 1832). ...It is a dangerous caricature of our Church to see it as a club whose members need permission from Rome to change their minds, or indeed to open their eyes, minds and hearts to new realities.

...The real scandal is still our divided Christianity. What really separates us is not so much faith, belief, or in many cases even theology, but rather entrenched attitudes and traditions that have little to do with the gospel. A basic principle of ecumenism is that the closer we come to Jesus, the closer we come to each other. The fact that we keep our distance so much from each other suggests that we should examine our consciences on how close we are to God. This would be a more fruitful exercise than publicly examining our President's conscience.

Conscience was primary for Seán. He took very seriously the Vatican II understanding of conscience as being that innermost self and was inviolable: "His conscience is man's [sic] most secret core, and his sanctuary". Allowing for the non-inclusive language that is still a feature of the Church, this makes an extremely important point. Seán emphasises the word 'sanctuary' which he says is:

...a sacred place, a place where God dwells, and should not be violated. This is why we respect people's consciences and why no one should ever be forced to act against his conscience.

He did not believe we should have just an *informed* conscience but a *formed* conscience. That distinction was everything, because it took into account the 'God-given' intelligence of the individual and their role in helping and contributing to the forming of conscience:

> This we have to do on the basis of our knowledge, experience and responsibility, and we are helped in our search by the laws of the community, by the guidance and teaching of our Church, by the advice of friends and expert counsellors when necessary...
>
> In discerning what is right or wrong in a situation, we must beware of prejudice, selfishness, selective attention to the facts, ignoring what does not suit us...
>
> All through life we must strive to form our conscience to keep it alive and healthy, delicately sensitive to moral values and the call of God.
>
> But when we fail and sin, there is no need to panic. The remedy is repentance, conversion, atonement. God's gift of forgiveness is always available.
>
> (Lenten reflection: *The Universe*, 20.03.81)

Seán deals with conscience in more depth in theological articles, but the above extract gets to the heart of the matter for him and makes it more accessible to the general reader.

It was because of this keen sense of always seeing the person, the fallible, sometimes broken human being held in the palm of the all-loving, all-merciful God, that the publisher, Michael Glazier, proposed the idea of a book on reconciliation to Seán in July 1999, and followed this up with a meeting in May 2000. Typically, Seán was not enthused by the idea of another book, but was willing to listen to the pitch from Michael. "I thought I had said everything I wanted to say in Chapter 9 of *Has Sin Changed?*" (PC 25.05.00). For Seán, a book was a means to convey your message, it was not an end in itself. No message, no book. Though Michael Glazier kept the idea in front of Seán for the next couple of years, he just could not muster the enthusiasm for it. He truly believed he said what he wanted or needed to say in *Has Sin Changed?* Also, there was the further complication that by this time, Sean's second book *Does Morality Change?* had been reported to the Vatican as not being in keeping with Catholic teaching (This will be dealt with in Chapter Five). There was some concern expressed by the European Provincial of the Marists that another book by Seán while the Vatican's doctrinal policing authority, the Congregation for the Doctrine of the Faith, had opened a case on *Does Morality Change?* might be problematic. However, this concern was not significant in Seán's thoughts about the book on reconciliation. He could stand over and justify everything he had written. He jotted a few ideas down and asked one or two people for their thoughts on the subject. If he felt he had anything useful to say, he would have written the book – ultimately, he did not.

Love rather than law

Though his particular expertise was in the area of sexual morality, Seán always considered morality in terms of the whole person in society, a society that has a particular history that must be admitted and owned. His broad knowledge of church history, canon law, philosophy, psychology, languages and more importantly, his knowledge and love of scripture, made his work more than the sum of its parts. This holistic approach meant that Seán was always in touch with those to whom he ministered, either directly or remotely through his writings. Though he possessed a very fine intellect, Seán never sought academic honour or advancement because he believed that his apostolate was to lighten the burdens (man-made or otherwise) of God's people, whether that was guilt, fear, loneliness, rejection, desperation or any of the other myriad miseries that beset people. Love rather than the Law was his guiding principle. For example, not long before Seán's physical health deteriorated sufficiently to restrict his mobility, he was a regular visitor to his friend Elizabeth Price in the UK. Elizabeth is actively involved in several reform groups that were close to Seán's heart – *Catholics for a Changing Church*, *Movement for Married Clergy* and *Dorcas*. *Dorcas* is a group that was set up by like-minded women after the promulgation of *Humanae Vitae* in 1968, banning 'artificial' means of birth control. It is named after a dedicated early Christian disciple – a woman who faithfully lived the Christian message. From its inception *Dorcas* had a letter-writing activism to the Catholic press, to priests and to bishops. It was a member of *Dorcas*, a retired librarian, disgusted at the treatment Seán was experiencing from the institutional Church, who suggested to Seán that he assign the copyright of his writings to an independent person, removed from the influence of the Marist Congregation and the Irish hierarchy. When Seán came back from this trip, he immediately contacted me and said he wanted me to take ownership of this copyright. Following several letters and proper legal advice, this was done.

When he stayed with Elizabeth, Seán was occasionally invited to say Mass in local churches if the resident priest was away. According to Elizabeth, "he is still talked about by those congregations on whom he made a deep impression as a spiritual and loving pastor". Seán visited one of Elizabeth's reflexology clients, a woman who was terminally ill. Later, following her death, Seán attended her memorial service which was conducted by an Irish woman, a priest in the Church of England. Impressed by the service, Seán, identifying himself as a Catholic priest, made sure to compliment her afterwards on the excellent sermon given. The woman wept and explained that she had been a cradle Catholic but felt the call to priesthood. Given the refusal of the Catholic Church to take seriously women's priestly vocations, she was obliged to move to the Church of England in order to respond to the call. This fulfilment of her vocation was also a source of great pain, as her mother has refused to speak to her since. Elizabeth said: "...so Seán's kindness was the more potent, and *so* typical of his way of sympathising with anyone in mental or spiritual pain" (PC/EP 15.04.18). His attitude can be summed up in a comment he had in his own retreat notes:

> I need to know and respond to God's purposes for me on a daily basis, to recognise his call inviting me to say *Yes* to the world, to myself, to my neighbours, to the whole of creation, and in all of this to God himself.

Seán practiced what he preached – his natural response was a consistent 'Yes' to service.

As a theologian, he made no claims to originality but, in the words of the late Austin Flannery OP, "he has used the findings of the best of the theological backroom boys, has shorn them of their jargon, and has made them accessible to the ordinary pastor, catechist and to the man and woman in the pew." This was Seán's special gift and he used it to the fullest in writing and broadcasting. Since he read widely, he had a significant reservoir of knowledge to draw upon. It is especially evident in his books *Has Sin Changed?* and *Does Morality Change?*, two extremely important books of adult formation on morality. Seán had no academic ambitions – he desired neither the acclaim nor the accolades that accompanied the ground-breaking work of the prominent theologians. Seán's enacting authority was the gospel message of love, compassion, hope and forgiveness and his ambition was to communicate that message to as many people as he could. He was utterly convinced by the necessity of the reforms of the Second Vatican Council, and was deeply concerned by the roll-back of these reforms during the papacies of John Paul II and Benedict XVI. His books did not contain extensive notes or bibliographies, simply because they were directed at an audience for whom these academic requirements were superfluous. Yet, their impact was such, the books ended up on reading lists of many theology courses. Though Seán was not an original theological thinker in terms of the big ideas and revolutionary thought, this is not to say his work was derivative. He brought his own intellect, wide reading and personality to bear on the source material so that his synthesis and use brought particular nuance to it. Anyone familiar with the sources can see their influence in Seán's work, but can also see the use he made of them.

In his two books Seán set out simply and clearly one of the greatest insights that has informed his theology through the years: the need to "relativise our false absolutes". While it might be invidious to attempt to summarise a person's life's work by one phrase, all of Seán Fagan's work, whether lecturing, broadcasting or writing has, in one way or another, been directed towards helping people to relativise their false absolutes. This has not just been directed at lay people, but also at church leadership, because the "lust for certainty" has led to much damage being caused to the church as people, and the church as institution. One way in which Seán brought this message was through a column he moderated in *The Universe* newspaper in the early 1980s.

CHAPTER THREE

The Universe story

The Universe newspaper was a popular, weekly UK Catholic newspaper founded in 1860. It was also sold in Ireland. Its readership reached a peak of over 300,000 in the 1960s and though it still had a significant readership of 95,000 by 1996, the circulation was, by then, falling rapidly and by the time of its sale to new owners at the turn of the millennium, it had declined to around 45,000. The Bishops of England & Wales held the controlling interest of 82% in the paper, which they sold in the early 2000s.

It was still a very popular, widely-read paper in July 1981 when Seán was asked to temporarily take over the *Family Matters* page, which had formerly been moderated by the Irishwoman, Angela McNamara. Seán was already an occasional contributor to the paper, doing a series of Lenten reflections in 1981. Even after his work with the *Family Matters* pages was completed, he still continued to contribute articles and reflections. In mid-July, 1986 when passing through London on his way from Rome to Dublin, he popped into the offices of *The Universe* for a courtesy call. The editor was in a panic because an article she had commissioned was unpublishable - it was too dull and not what was expected - and the paper was going to press the following day. She asked if Seán could do something... anything... to get her out of the crisis. All he had was a "broken-down, antique typewriter in a corner of the office," and he produced the article in an hour. The article was called *Nobody grows alone* and is one of three that remained his favourites of all that he had written. (The other two being *Sacraments in the spiritual life* and *It's good to be here,* mentioned earlier). It was no small feat to produce it as he did, from scratch, under pressure. But this was typical of Seán's attitude – if someone needed help and he was in a position to offer it, he did, regardless of the demands on his time.

The 'few weeks' in charge of *Family Matters* stretched into two years as he dealt with readers' problems on a variety of issues, most of which were faith and church matters. Given that he had also studied psychology, he was quite comfortable taking on the role. Seán made the decision to write under a pseudonym, Anne Egan, thinking that the readership was already used to a woman, and might feel intimated by a priest being in charge. A little more than three months later on 6th November, 1981, an irate reader wrote to the *Family Matters* stating she or he (no names were published) had:

> ...noticed a change in the kind of letters published and the replies you give. ...You seem to wander into spiritual matters and psychological problems that should be dealt with by specialists.
>
> The cobbler should stick to his last. An individual trained to deal with material social problems is not normally qualified to deal with spiritual or moral social problems.
>
> Priests, nuns and legionaries are specially trained and they have a mandate by virtue of their office for these problems. At least legionaries can channel problems outside their particular field to specially qualified people.

From the letter, one imagines the writer to be a member of the Legion of Mary, but perhaps not. Seán gently assured the reader that he had over 30 years international experience of counselling and that he regularly consulted sources of other expertise. But he continues to make the most important point:

The main reason why I publish this letter [from the complainant] is to make the point that an advice column like this is simply an emergency service.

In the Christian community, we are our brother's keeper. Those of us in trouble should be able to reach out for help to an immediate neighbour without always waiting for the specialist.

As Christians, all of us should be able to help at least in caring and being concerned.

The fact that special problems need professional help should not prevent us from helping personally in whatever small way we can.

Remember Our Lord's words to his disciples: "even a cup of water…"

However, to assuage the worries of the more scrupulous readership, a notice was published on the page during January 1982 that Anne Egan was now joined by 'Fr Paul' to assist in the more weighty answers that required theological heft. All theological questions were to be addressed to him. Of course, Fr Paul was Seán Fagan. So despite the orthodoxy and good sense of Anne Egan, for a certain cohort of readers, it only became acceptable when this was mediated through the priest, Fr Paul.

From the perspective of history, reading a wide selection from the letters to *Family Matters* over the period Seán was involved with the paper offers an interesting glimpse into the preoccupations of Catholics at the time. Without doing a scientific analysis, the main concerns were: Catholics marrying divorced people; younger people walking away from the Church; Catholics marrying people from other denominations or faith traditions. Most of the letters were from people doing their very best to struggle with things they had difficulty understanding, trying to see both sides of the argument.

However, there was a small but steady number of letters from people very angry about the changes that Vatican II brought about. For most of these people 'church teaching' was a static thing that brooked no attenuation, modification or, heaven forfend, change. Some of them were aghast that hell was not being spoken of with the same fervour as before, others that the Church was going soft on excommunication.

Seán dealt with these people gently but firmly, pointing out much of what they understood to be immutable church teaching was actually more habit and convention that had gathered over time. He further helped the readers by doing short book reviews of what he considered useful sources to help broaden their thinking, their horizons and their understanding of the Church.

Another concern of many *Universe* readers was the 'protestantisation' of the Church. More than a few correspondents were very perturbed by this tendency. For instance, one letter-writer thought that the "traditional dogmas and doctrines of the Church will need to be repeated and confirmed by a Third Vatican Council". She or he was very disturbed by the prominence given to scripture in the Mass, and hoped that a new Council would see to it that "...people would be encouraged to do the greater part of their reading of the scriptures in their own homes so that they can spend more time at Mass worshipping God".

There is a definite pattern that those people who had difficulty with change, feared 'protestantisation' and felt the penalties of the Church were not being applied severely enough, also had major difficulty with the Mass as table fellowship and as thanksgiving. For them, Mass was a sacrifice only. Their certitudes were worn with pride and they seemed to believe they had a moral obligation to tell other people where they were going wrong. Of course, the certitudes were not supported by any evidence other than opinion. And there appeared to be no understanding that they had anything to learn.

Hellfire and brimstone

The teaching on hell caused quite a stir. This was in the issue of 20th November, 1981, as a conclusion to Seán's reply to a correspondent on the reality or otherwise of an angry punishing God, who would hurt the innocent and blameless to "appease divine justice". The letter-writer repudiated the idea of such a God, and Seán affirmed the sensible attitude of this person. In his concluding words Seán spoke of hell:

> As for hell, it is not a place of torment created by God to punish people for their sins, but rather that state of *spiritual* isolation and inversion suffered by people who have definitively and irrevocably shut God out of their lives, rejected him.
>
> They become so turned in on self that they lose the capacity to love. There is no greater hell than this, and part of the torment is the knowledge that we ourselves are the cause of it.

A correspondent in the issue of 25th December, 1981, quoted from the reading of the feast of Christ the King (last Sunday of the Church's liturgical year, just before the beginning of Advent) where Jesus says that sinners "will go away to eternal punishment". And then inquires if columnist [Seán in the guise of Anne Egan] has "...some private revelation denied to the rest of us? I prefer to stick to the original and authoritative version". Bear in mind that people believed they were writing to a lay woman. Seán reassures the rather miffed correspondent that he has no special revelation, but that he consulted the work of Karl Rahner's *Concise Theological Dictionary*, (despite its title it is a rather substantial work), which had its imprimatur from the Diocese of Westminster (i.e., it is in keeping with the teaching of the Catholic Church). This says that hell is a popular expression for the failure to reach the presence of God (heaven) and the final consequences of the state of final personal alienation from God.

This brought a reaction from another correspondent, published on 29th January, 1982, who asked:

> Why do you persist in rejecting the traditional doctrine of Hell as taught by the Church for nearly 2,000 years...

> What you have been presenting are merely theological *opinions,* not the official teaching of the Church. Instead of quoting doubtful theologians like Rahner, why not write to the Holy See and ask our present Holy Father whether the official teaching has been changed?

Karl Rahner was one of the giants of the Church and one of the most important theologians of the 20th Century. To describe him as 'doubtful' would be like describing Einstein as a dubious theoretical mathematician.

For some people, such as our letter-writer above, the desire for eternal damnation and punishment by eternal flames seemed very important indeed. Nothing less would do. To be deprived of the presence of God wasn't hell enough. Again, gently but very firmly, Seán, quoting from the most recent teaching on matters of heaven and hell, put the letter-writer straight. He quoted from the then most recent document on eschatology (the study of last things – death, judgement, heaven, hell and purgatory) approved by John Paul II in 1979. "We must therefore provide them with the means to be firm with regard to the essence of the doctrine (of the eschaton) and at the same time careful not to allow childish or arbitrary images to be considered truths of faith."

It is interesting to note that Seán began his reply as follows:

> I was absolutely amazed at the volume of correspondence that has come in on the subject of hell. When trying to answer

a reader's query about the subject a few weeks ago, I never realised that so many people feel so strongly about it.

A few writers advised me to stick to family problems and leave such subjects to qualified experts.

On 19th February, 1982, obviously missing the earlier notification of the arrival of Fr Paul as advisor, another letter-writer joined the discussion, wondering what qualifications Anne Egan had for expounding Catholic doctrine in *The Universe*; in itself, not an unreasonable question. But in his or her anger, the correspondent showed much the same difficulties with change as those mentioned above, and declared that "there is a real danger of *Universe* readers being seriously misled with regard to the teaching of the Church and some correction should be published to avoid this". Enter Fr Paul, again, to whom questions of a theological nature could be addressed.

One cannot help but wonder why, when the doctrine of last things was considered in a more sensible and theologically proper way, did so many people object to the presentation of hell as the absence of God. Why had they such a need to hold on to the punishment of damnation to eternal flames? Was the personal choice and responsibility involved in the more proper presentation of hell too much of a moral challenge? Was it easier to believe in an angry God who had to be appeased, rather than make the daily decisions of how to be moral in all aspects of our behaviour and dealings with others? It certainly speaks to the poor state of adult formation in the Church even in the early 1980s.

The people of certainty, who applied the term 'church teaching' to every opinion without discretion were fewer in number than the general type of correspondent trying to find a way through a world that was changing rapidly, both inside and outside the Church. There were questions about organ transplants, cremation, in-vitro fertilization and so forth, where the person querying it put much thought and effort into trying to come to a conclusion. Given the complexities of some of the queries and the limitations of space in the newspaper, Seán, nevertheless managed a good deal of solid adult formation for anyone truly willing to learn.

Sensitive to the vulnerable

Apart from a search for meaning or direction, a sense of loneliness came through in some of the letters, but with it sense of community as other correspondents wrote in with helpful suggestions. Seán understood the importance of selecting such letters for publication. One that was particularly heartening in its practical good sense, was a response to a very lonely widow who wrote in early December 1982 about the crushing loneliness after the recent death of her husband. Her children lived far away, and though neighbours were kind, the visits had tapered off. She saw a future stretching ahead of her looking very empty and bleak. A few weeks later another woman wrote in to suggest a course of action she had taken. She was sitting alone one evening and realised that there had to be other people in the same lonely situation as herself. She approached her parish priest with the idea of an open letter which would be distributed after all the Masses, inviting all those who had lost loved ones to a meeting. Out of this was born a group for people in similar circumstances who understood each other. Once a month they were invited to a member's home where they would spend the day together. For parish events, they requested that a table be set aside for the group. Whereas prior to this, people did not go to functions alone, now they had each other and would go all events.

The nature of the *Family Matters* page (lots of letters, very little space) meant that many letters were not published. Also, it limited the extent of the responses by 'Anne' or 'Fr Paul' to particular queries, which sometimes resulted in very annoyed letters, similar to those quoted above on hell and punishment. But overall, *The*

66

Universe was a useful conduit to reach many people with excellent catechesis they might not otherwise have received. This points to another important matter – how an emotionally vulnerable person is treated when they approach a priest. Several times during the two years of Seán's moderation of the *Family Matters* page, correspondents spoke of the reception they received from a priest – some, with good pastoral instincts, showed great kindness and understanding which gave great solace. Other priests, similar to the people full of certainty mentioned above, responded with callousness and disdain. All correspondents to *Family Matters* were treated with respect and gentleness by Seán, even those who were less than gracious in their letters. He understood, as Gerard Hughes SJ did in his classic *God of Surprises*, that within Catholicism just like other Christian denominations, there were those who "have opened the treasure and live with the life it provides" while there are those "who are still sitting on closed boxes, alarmed and afraid, and condemning those who show signs of a new life in Christ" (*God of Surprises*, p.114).

A notable feature of Seán's replies was the consistency with which he presented Church teaching in his responses. Vatican II was his point of reference always and where teaching seemed difficult and cold-hearted, he nuanced it through his own faith and formal knowledge. Not only did he deal with the letters published, Seán also entered into a private follow-up correspondence counselling service with many people. He wrote between 600-700 letters a year, on a portable Smith-Corona typewriter. This was before email or computers with word processing applications. It was done in the spare time he found from full-time teaching, article writing and the manual maintenance work he did around the Marist house in Mount St Mary's, Milltown, Dublin.

He said that most people who knew him imagine that he was a workaholic "...but the reality is not quite like that. I like to get things done, especially for others. I do them quickly and efficiently (and get a kick out of it, both from the job done and helping others), but often I get things done just to get onto the next item! ... I like the final sentence of Bernarnos' novel *Diary of a Country Priest* – 'tout est grâce' (unfortunately wrongly translated in English as 'grace is everywhere'. The original is: Everything is grace)" (PC 07.02.00). It was this concept of 'everything is grace' that propelled Seán in all that he did. Whether that was his manual work with carpentry, minor electrical or plumbing problems, in dressmaking - he made several albs and stoles – or his theological and pastoral work. As he said to me: *le style c'est l'homme.*

CHAPTER FOUR

Two (three) books

Any attempt to analyse or assess Seán Fagan's writings to search for meaning is not a useful exercise, because the clarity of his thought and his crisp prose style mean that everything he has to say is laid out, accessible to all. Everything he has to say is relevant to his topic; he says it with an economy of words and clarity of expression that makes his books page-turners, something rare in theological publishing.

His first book *Has Sin Changed?* grew out of a short article called 'No more sin?' that was published in *Doctrine & Life* in June 1976. But it had its first airing in a public lecture given in the Milltown Institute in 1965. It informed an interview he did for the programme *Encounter* with RTÉ television in 1974. One radio/TV reviewer said "I should dearly wish to have the space to quote the whole interview, and let it speak for itself," and then devoted almost all his column space to the review of *Encounter*. (Tom O'Dea, 'Critics on Saturday,' *The Irish Press*, 27th April 1974)

Has Sin Changed?

The 'No more sin?' article was reprinted without permission in an American publication, *Catholic Mind* in January 1977, though *Doctrine & Life* was acknowledged as the source. Unable to sleep one night, the highly-regarded liturgical publisher, Michael Glazier, a Kerryman living in the United States, picked up the magazine and was overwhelmed by 'No more sin?' when he read it. He tracked down Seán Fagan, and told him he would like to see the article expanded and turned into a book. Seán's first reaction was "I am a hundred yards dash man. I write articles, I don't think I can write a book." Thankfully, Michael Glazier understood the importance of the expansion of the ideas contained in the article and was able to persuade him otherwise. *Has Sin Changed?*, written on his portable Smith-Corona in just two months, appeared on the bookshelves in 1977. Previously, Seán's doctor had instructed him to cancel all his retreat work and lectures that summer because his health had suffered due to overwork. He did as he was told, cancelled his commitments, stayed at home and wrote a book instead. He sent it to the US chapter by chapter as it was written. According to the publisher, those involved in the set-up of the text for printing were so taken by it that they eagerly awaited each new chapter, like following a serial in a magazine (PC 26.09.99).

It was chosen by the Thomas More Society for their book-of-the-month club. In the US it was a talking book for the blind. In 1979 Doubleday of New York brought out a special edition, with a run of 50,000 copies, to celebrate the 25th anniversary of their imprint, Image Books. It sold over 65,000 copies worldwide, unusual for a religious book. It was the first theological book published by Michael Glazier, Inc., but his firm soon became one of the foremost publishers of Catholic theology in the English-speaking world, and a by-word for high quality books.

One American reviewer, Paul H. Hallett, gave *Has Sin Changed?* a short but very negative review in the *National Catholic Register* (26.02.78), where he was a contributing editor. Hallett would have been considered a particularly vociferous, ultra-conservative Catholic. He ended the review by writing: "The book is reviewed here only to warn those who may still think of Ireland as an impregnable citadel of orthodoxy." Michael Glazier felt the review was unfair and had not judged the book on its own merits, and wrote to Hallett listing his concerns. Hallett then wrote a much more extensive negative review in the edition of 23rd April, 1978. Contrary to Mr Hallett's intention to warn people away from reading *Has Sin Changed?* his longer review had the effect of boosting sales of the book.

A common theme in all the reviews of the book, including the review by Hallett, was the clarity of the ideas and the accessible language through which they were expressed.

Creating a stir

Has Sin Changed? created quite a stir in Ireland and elsewhere. This was at a time when morality was seen much more in terms of sin and retribution and of obeying the rules rather than as a freely-chosen responsibility. This was also a time when it seemed that the only real sin in the Catholic Church was sexual sin. *Has Sin Changed?* was a book that called for a completely new approach to sin and captured something of the Vatican II zeitgeist. It used a well thought out adult approach that saw sin in the context of life choices and behaviour, rather than the childish, simplistic notion of rewards and punishment. It tackled the subject under a number of clear headings:

What happened to sin?
What does the Bible say?
Is it allowed?
How far can I go?
How sinful is sex?
My conscience or the law?
Am I really guilty?
Does God punish sin?
God's gift of forgiveness
Can morality be taught?
Let's rehabilitate sin!

It is difficult to single out any chapter as being central to the book since they follow each other logically, developing the thought that we, as adults, have to take responsibility for our moral growth and form our consciences accordingly. We cannot abdicate that responsibility by simply conforming to a pre-ordained set of rules and regulations. As a reviewer in the *Irish Catechist* said: "[this book] deserves to be read in every presbytery and publicised in every pulpit, and the more controversy it engenders in every house, private and even public, the clearer our grasp of the answer it gives to the question it asks."

Gabriel Fallon reviewed it for the *Irish Independent* in May 1978. Fallon was a widely-read, intelligent and thinking man who was not easily intimidated by the might of the Church. He had good and bad experiences in intellectual exchanges with individual priests. Though he was unembittered by the negative experiences, nevertheless, he was quite sceptical of clerical authors. He was almost 80 years old at the time of the review and said that he "learned more concerning God and man from poets and playwrights, weighed against my own life experience, than I learned from many a pulpit". However, he was delighted with *Has Sin Changed?* and finished his review by declaring, "This is a book which should be in the hands of every priest, religious leader and parent who takes his or her vocation seriously." (*Irish Independent* 08.05.78)

Even though in some respects it was a book of a particular era, and geared to the general reader, whether clerical or lay, it has stood the test of time remarkably well. It bears re-reading, especially as there seems to be a concerted attempt, despite the efforts of Pope Francis, within the Church leadership to return to an inward-looking institution, hidebound by rules that admit no dissent. The Church Seán envisaged in his book as having "much fewer and far less detailed moral rules than in the past, and will focus more on funda-mental principles of moral reasoning, deeper insight into human and

Christian values, and a heightened sense of personal responsibility among the faithful", seems more of a distant dream now, more than 40 years later, than it did in 1978.

Much to his amazement, and pleasure, Seán occasionally received reactions to *Has Sin Changed?* many years after publication. One such was in 1999, when "an agnostic English computer expert who is married to a very fine Vietnamese Catholic woman" became a Catholic after reading *Does Morality Change?* and was trying to find a copy of *Has Sin Changed?* As by then the book was out of print, he wrote to Seán to try and get a copy. Seán had no spares to give away, so photocopied the whole book for his new-found convert. Nothing that contributed to the education of 'God's holy people' was too much work for him.

Does Morality Change?

Seán's second book *Does Morality Change?* written in just three months, and first published in 1997 by Gill & Macmillan, is probably even more important than his first. While it is inevitable that he covers some of the same ground, this book is much broader in its scope and more comprehensive in its treatment of morality. He tackles the subject under headings that need no explanation:

Confused by change
Life is change
What is morality?
Morality and religion
Does nature change?
Conscience today
Moral discernment
Responsible parenthood
Church teaching
New challenges

Again, it would be difficult to pick out a central focus of this book, although perhaps the chapters on conscience and moral discernment are the core chapters from which everything else radiates.

> Morality is about choice... what is the morally right thing to do? ...But conscience is more than just decision. ...It calls to something deep within our nature, and leaves us with the conviction that we must obey it if we are to be true to ourselves. In this sense, conscience is more than just intellect and will, knowledge and consent. On this deepest of all levels, conscience is the core of our being as free persons.
>
> ...Morally mature people know their own limitations and weakness, but are constantly open to new information, new insights, new values and they want to grow in sensitivity and willingness to do good.
>
> (*Does Morality Change?* 2nd edn Dublin: Columba Press, 2003, pp.121-26)

Seán's willingness to inform people and then trust them with the results of that information is the striking feature of *Does Morality Change?* He is an educator in the fullest meaning of the word. He leads us out of confusion and misunderstanding, out of a childish notion of morality, points the way towards an adult acceptance of responsibility, then stands back and trusts us to use that knowledge well. "If you are going to trust people, then trust them" was an oft-repeated saying of his.

Given that it was on the reading lists of many third-level moral theology courses around the world, and remains relevant for any Catholic interested in an adult faith, it is no surprise that *Does Morality Change?* went out of print within three years. (I heard one story where a lecturer in an adult education course, in desperation, made 12 photocopies of the entire book because it was out of print – the morality of flouting copyright law wasn't discussed!). The late Seán O'Boyle, who served the Irish Church well through The Columba Press publishing house, saw the place and value of *Does Morality Change?* within Ireland. He approached Seán about publishing a second edition. The book appeared on the shelves in 2003 - a fitting tribute to Seán in his Golden Jubilee of Ordination year. *Does Morality Change?* could simply have been reprinted as it was, but true to form, Seán felt it necessary to modify the text to include some words on the clerical sexual abuse scandals and is typically forthright:

> The abuse cases have alerted us to the need for a radical examination of the clerical culture that enabled them to occur and the mindset which prompted the disastrous attempts at cover-up. ...The recent revelations may have rocked the faith of Catholics, but they can also be the catalyst that will open the way to true reform. A healthy change for the Church would be to relinquish the triumphalism of the past and discover that God may be closer to us in our humiliation.
>
> (*Does Morality Change?* p.21)

Motivation

Seán's motivation for writing sprang from his own spirituality and from his deep pastoral instincts. It reflected the kindness and compassion of Jesus as portrayed in the gospels. With that kindness and compassion there was also a steely determination to call to account those in power who mediated a harsh and unforgiving Church. Seán's constant mission was to help people understand the prodigality of God's love – we all matter, we are all loved by God without reference to privilege or status.

It was this compassion and inclusiveness that informed all Seán's actions – in his bones he believed utterly that we are all Church. For Seán, the exclusion of wider *ecclesia* from decision-making made a mockery of the inclusiveness articulated at Vatican II. In 1987 he cast a jaundiced eye at the Synod of Bishops on the vocation and mission of laity, pointing out that:

> As subjects they are excluded in principle, and no amount of 'consultation' can alter this fact. ...Consultation is simply not enough. Those consulting decide on the topic, its scope, degree of detail, duration and timing of the consultation, and then filter and summarise the results to fit a pre-decided conclusion...

> (*Doctrine & Life*, Jan 1987)

Seán always believed in the importance of communication and consultation within the Church at large. He followed the example of Newman, who challenged Bishop Ullathorne who did not want the laity 'disturbed'. Ullathorne was quite cross that *The Rambler*, a progressive Catholic periodical edited for a short time by Newman, was still showing the "remains of the old spirit", i.e., challenging the hierarchy. In this instance Newman had warned the bishops to "really desire to know the opinion of the laity on subjects in which the laity are especially concerned". He concluded his article by warning against "the misery of any division between the rulers of the Church and the educated laity". The bishop rather grumpily asked "Who are the laity?" Newman replied: "The Church would look foolish without them." (*Letters & Diaries of JHN*, Vol xix, pp.140-1) [cited in Ker, *John Henry Newman* pp.478-9].

Responses

It is hardly surprising that *Does Morality Change?* was well received critically and reviews were positive. It did not make the same media impact as *Has Sin Changed?* but that is more for reasons of culture and education than anything else. However, many individuals (locally and worldwide) took the time and trouble to write to the author expressing their feelings. Two representative reactions to *Does Morality Change?* come from a woman in her late sixties and an American Jesuit priest. The woman says:

> As a 'recovering Catholic' I want to thank you from the heart for your book *Does Morality Change?* and for the healing it's bringing to me in my late sixties. Thanks to people like yourself ...liberation day has come and mindsets are changing (my own big time). Most of my life has been slavery, keeping rules, etc. All along my heart knew I was just a hypocrite but was led to believe it was a 'sin' to question the Church, so I did my 'duty' faithfully and nearly perfectly! My sick body paid the price. I won't go on ... another outburst of anger isn't too far away! Thanks again for your great courage and for bringing us the *truth* that does set us free.

The Jesuit priest says:

> I have read and reread your excellent book. I have recommended it to many friends, although I must admit that when I first came across it two or three years ago I was not inclined to either read it or buy it. My thinking was as follows: written by an Irish theologian, and worse still, one who had lived for many years in Rome; must be all bad, even pre-Trent! But then I saw the dedication to my two favourite moral theologians, Bernard Häring and Richard McCormick. I then bought it and treasure it. Please continue your great work. With the death of Richard McCormick and Bernard Häring in recent years we are sadly lacking in truly great moral theologians. You and Charles Curran and very few others remain to guide us in the world of moral theology.

Collision course

It seems almost counter-intuitive that Seán's sense of the boundless compassion of God, of the value each one of us has in the sight of that loving God, the Church as mustard tree – the symbol of Christian inclusiveness, should be what brought him into conflict with the Church authorities. But that is what happened. Seán wasn't a maverick, who sought attention for its own sake. His outspokenness came not from being an outsider, beating his own drum, but from being very much an insider with a deep understanding of the institution to which he faithfully committed just over 70 years by the time of his death in 2016. In 1994 he said:

> ...An objective study of church history is a sobering experience, showing how often the institutional elements hindered or even stifled the Spirit. It is no service to truth to ignore such attitudes and actions.

> ...church leadership, in prayerful consultation with the rest of the faithful, has the task of discerning the gifts, testing the spirits to see if the new initiatives are from God, but their discernment will be seriously defective unless they have a firm conviction that the charismatic reality of religious life is an essential part of the life and holiness of the Church. For their part, religious ...must remain true to their vocation to be spearheads, pioneers, Kingdom-spotters, even when it means being a thorn in the side of those whose charism is to discern and co-ordinate. ...We need each other."

> (*Religious Life Review,* Mar-Apr 1994, pp.66-75)

It is worth noting here that two of Seán's heroes, Bernard Häring CSsR and Richard McCormick, SJ, very significant figures in 20th Century moral theology, both admitted that they needed to re-think some of their earlier work – Häring, because he felt he'd been too cautions in not wanting to challenge the ruling class within the Church, McCormick because he believed that he'd uncritically followed the laws and teachings of the Church, and experience had taught him that life does not fit neatly into the package of laws and rules. Seán, because of his common sense approach and ongoing self-education, did not find himself needing to revise his attitudes nor apply corrective vision.

The reason for the (three) in parenthesis in the title of this chapter is that Seán brought out a third book, *What Happened to Sin?*. This was not a new book, but an updated version of his first book, *Has Sin Changed?*. But this book barely saw the light of day. It was removed from sale and public access within 18 months of its publication. The reason for this will be explained in Chapter Seven.

CHAPTER FIVE

Accusations

Seán Fagan first came to the attention of the Vatican's Congregation for the Doctrine of the Faith (CDF) in December 1998 for his second book *Does Morality Change?* which was published the previous year. The then secretary of the CDF, Archbishop Tarcisio Bertone, wrote to the superior general of the Marists to tell him that the book had been denounced to the CDF as not in keeping with Church teaching.

The Congregation for the Doctrine of the Faith (CDF)

It is worth noting here that the CDF is a direct descendant of the Roman Inquisition set up in 1542 during the Reformation period. It was comprised of cardinals, bishops and archbishops without any lay or female involvement until April 2018 when Pope Francis appointed three women to this dicastery. The person in charge of the department is called the Prefect. It has an office staff and a list of regular consultors. These consultors are the people who read and critique work that is under scrutiny by the CDF. To date they have all been men and all clerics. The consultors are not named, but the majority have taught in pontifical universities in Rome. Given the anonymity, it is difficult to assess any consultor's credentials for commentary on theological writings. They may teach, but do they write? Are they up to date in their reading of theology? Have they presented their opinions within the theological environment for critique? Do they belong to one particular 'school' of theology? This is very important, as I will point out later.

Of the CDF's investigative methods, the former Archbishop Roberts SJ of Bombay stated in 1963 that he did not see any difference in how the Holy Office [as the CDF was called then] conducted itself compared to the Inquisitions of the Middle Ages. He said while it was more difficult to kill and imprison those whom it regarded as troublesome, "reputations are ruined and careers are broken". This was as true when Seán Fagan was punished, as it was in 1963 when Archbishop Roberts uttered the words. And it remains true today, despite Pope Francis' exhortation to theologians and others not to be worried about the office, because it is just biding its time waiting to spring to life again under a sympathetic pope.

Anonymous accuser

Does Morality Change? was denounced to the CDF by somebody as not in keeping with Catholic teaching. This is called being 'delated' to Rome. A theologian is delated when his or her work is accused of having doctrinal errors and to contain dangerous opinions and reported to the doctrinal watchdog of the Vatican. Such delations can come from a local bishop, but certain lay groups who cling to a rigid hyper-orthodoxy have delated theologians. Individuals can also delate a theologian on foot of writings or lectures. These writings can be as simple as a Letter to the Editor of a respected newspaper or a lecture given to a private group.

Observations

Seán was never given the name of his accuser, nor offered the opportunity to face them. We do not know if it was a person with a theological background or a person with the mindset of some of the writers to *The Universe* who had tremendous difficulty coming to terms with the changes ushered in by Vatican II. Instead, the superior general of the Marist congregation was sent a letter accompanied by an 11-page set of *Observations* on the book compiled by a consultor to the CDF. When I first read the CDF's accusations against Seán in the *Observations*, I simply did not recognise *Does Morality Change?* as the book under scrutiny.

It is interesting to note here the experience of the eminent theologian Elizabeth Johnson, CSJ. When responding to criticism of her excellent book, *Quest for the living God*, by the doctrinal committee of the United States Conference of Catholic Bishops, Sr Elizabeth says of some of the critique:

> It takes sentences and, despite my clarifications to the contrary, makes them conclude to positions that I have not taken and would never take. The committee's reading projects meanings, discovers insinuations, and otherwise distorts the text so that in some instances I do not recognise the book I wrote.

Seán was accused of:
- Reductive and pervasive historicism
- Relativism
- Problematic presentation of natural law
- Attitude towards the Magisterium
- Autonomy of conscience without due reference to Catholic teaching
- Proportionalism and rejection of *Veritatis Splendor*

In principle, I do not think anybody would argue with the right of the teaching authority of the Church to challenge what it perceives as faulty interpretation of its teaching. However, one would hope that such a challenge would, at a minimum, not attempt to misrepresent that interpretation. The opening sentence of the accusation is:

The fundamental aim of this book is to argue for alteration and change in the moral teaching of the Catholic Church.

This sets the tone for what follows throughout the whole document. Apart from being a rash judgment, it is manifestly untrue. As Seán specifically states on p.206 of the first edition:

The purpose of this book was not to score points off fellow theologians or to ruffle the feathers of some bishops (who have a difficult enough time at the present), but rather the pastoral concern to help people feel at home in a Church which respects their God-given intelligence as well as calling on their loyalty and piety.

And this is the purpose of the book that I and several thousand others read, and what we took from it. I worked with students in a distance education programme in theology and *Does Morality Change?* was on the reading list for the moral theology module. Where expressed to me, the response from students to this book was consistent – it made great sense in the light of their experience, its information was easily accessed and the concepts explained easily understood. Many found it more than just helpful in the academic sense, they also found it very consoling in a spiritual sense.

Response

Seán ably rebutted the CDF's claims, showing how its arguments frequently took statements out of context within the book. For example, Seán makes it clear that moral teachings do, in fact, change in time and also explained the shift from a classicist method in theology to an historical consciousness method. But he did not canonise historical consciousness in the process. The CDF document adopts a dismissive attitude to this important change in theological method

– a change which was very evident at Vatican II and in the subsequent documents of the Council. The CDF document does not make any argument as to why historical consciousness is not an acceptable premise for moral evaluation and development. But instead it says:

> The consequence of the author's commitment to such an understanding of historical consciousness is a relativistic understanding of truth, including doctrinal truth as taught by the universal magisterium. [And it is] then but a short step to call into questions the notion that there exists a 'deposit of faith'.

The document says 'a short step', but what a giant leap it makes in its accusations. Seán makes no such claim in *Does Morality Change?*. Rather, he points out that not everything taught previously belongs to the 'deposit of faith'. But this type of unfair claim characterises the whole case against Seán Fagan. Indeed, the consultor shows no awareness that the term 'deposit of faith' did not appear in the Church vocabulary until the Council of Trent in the 16th Century. It only came into common use in the 19th Century during the papacy of Pius IX who saw himself as an embattled prisoner of the Vatican, standing against anything that might threaten Catholic orthodoxy. The term 'deposit of faith' was a blunt instrument used to challenge the questioning of previously held assumptions. Prior to, during and following Vatican II, there was a return to the previously long-held tradition of the deposit of faith as something dynamic – the life, death and resurrection of Christ was not a one-time event held forever static in the amber of time, rather it lives on in the tradition of the Church. The deposit of faith does not exist outside history, impervious to the change arising from philosophy and from human and natural sciences. This interpretation of the 'deposit of faith' that Seán understood is consistent with the teaching of the Church.

Seán answered the CDF's claims, point for point in his 10-page response. The following will give a flavour of his response. He challenged the charge of "reductive and pervasive historicism" by pointing out the "the important distinction so clearly expressed by Pope John XXIII between the substance of Church teaching and its formulation or expression in different times and cultures". He notes that the criticism of his work "seems to imply that there is a Church teaching which is a-temporal, a-historical, a-cultural, and in this sense totally 'objective'". He points out that this is impossible, that even God's word in the Bible is expressed in human words, in different languages and as such, can never be a-historical or a-cultural: "Hence the need for hermeneutics and exegesis".

He challenged the negative attitude towards the move from classical method to historical consciousness, pointing out that this shift was widely accepted within academic circles. Its implications for theology and philosophy "were widely discussed and publicised for decades by the Canadian Jesuit Bernard Lonergan, a long-time professor at the Gregorian University" in Rome. Seán made clear that moral teachings do, in fact, change over time and also explained the shift from the classicist method in theology to a historical consciousness method.

He pointed out that most of the material of the Ten Commandments was already found in law codes of the surrounding ancient Near East cultures prior to their being written down in Hebrew scripture. He observed that in the New Testament, Jesus did not leave a detailed code of morality to his followers, so Paul and the early Christian communities used the codes of their own environment, in this case Greek knowledge of virtues and vices. The difference was the new context in how these were understood: either giving life in the Spirit or opposing life in the Spirit. He comments that even the New Testament does not supply "a direct and simple answer to modern problems like inflation and poverty, racial conflict, social justice, birth control, genetic engineering, etc.".

On the charge of relativism he quotes the Vatican II document on revelation, *Dei Verbum* n.10 and states his acceptance that "scripture and tradition make up a single deposit of the world of God". He also points out that *Dei Verbum* makes clear that while the magisterium of the Church has the responsibility of authentic interpretation of the deposit of faith, it is not superior to it, rather it is its servant. He then points out that to include in the 'deposit of faith' everything taught by the Church down through the centuries "creates serious difficulties for modern Catholics". For example, "Pius IX, echoing Gregory XVI, could declare that freedom of conscience was sheer madness, an erroneous and absurd opinion, while John XXIII and the fathers of Vatican II ...proclaimed it a basic human right." He also spoke of the development of human freedom and dignity. "Slavery could be accepted without question by St Paul and even defended philosophically by Aquinas, whereas the very idea of slavery is abhorrent to people today, and this is reflected in Church teaching."

On absolute moral norms, he makes the point that "the moral commandments to be loving, just, truthful, honest, chaste, merciful, etc., are unchanging, and have an absolute normative character. But when it comes to defining the kinds of behaviour that qualify as loving, just, etc., there can be changes". And he quoted Thomas Aquinas who says that in moral matters the more one descends from general principles to specific cases there is less clarity and certainty on what must be done in a given situation.

Seán's mission pastorally and pedagogically was to "relativise our false absolutes". This was not to say there were no absolutes; he never claimed that, but that those absolutes are few, fundamental and should be handled with care. As Seán pointed out to the consultor in his reply:

> The inspired word of God can give us guidance, values and principles for the analysis and solution of these problems, but

if the concrete solution could be found simply by reading the Bible, there would be no need for moral discernment by the individual conscience, the Christian community or the teaching of the Church.

The propensity to selectively quote, out of context, from *Does Morality Change?* and then to accuse Seán on this flawed basis is a consistent feature of the consultor's *Observations*. The same thing happens with Seán's treatment of conscience. The consultor accuses Seán of encouraging "an autonomous understanding of conscience detached from proper formation in objective morality as known through recourse to Catholic teaching". This is a complete misrepresentation of Seán's action and intent. A misrepresentation bordering on malicious, as one assumes some theological competence on the part of the consultor, therefore ignorance of the topic is hardly an excuse.

Seán consistently spoke of a 'formed' conscience, which requires plenty of effort and hard work on the part of the individual. The individual cannot abdicate personal responsibility by just relying on "what the Church says", because anyone with any interest in Church history and doctrinal development and change knows, rules *do* change. There may be those who refuse to admit this fact, and engage in reform by amnesia – but as another of Seán's sayings tells us "*contra factum, non argumentum*".

CDF's procedures

It is worth noting here that there was never any response given to Seán on his point-by-point rebuttal of the consultor's accusations in the *Observations*. Instead, in April 1999, the then superior general of the Marists, Fr Jan Hulshof, received a letter from the CDF telling him that Seán did not accept the comments of the consultor and therefore must appear before the doctrinal tribunal of the Vatican to be interrogated in person. Sean's religious superiors were quite upset about this, but nothing further happened in the months following the April communication. There was no summons to a tribunal. Then, a year later, in April 2000, the Marist superior general received correspondence telling him that in their meeting of 19th January, 2000, the CDF took the decision to forward Seán's case to the Irish Episcopal Conference rather than dealing with it themselves. The Irish bishops were ordered to publish a *Notification* (a warning) about the book. It would appear that they were not asked to examine the book and decide if there was a case to be answered – they were treated like regional managers of a large global conglomerate. They were given an order to be carried out. This is another aspect of the case which raises significant theological and ecclesiological questions – the authority of the bishops of the local churches and the principle of subsidiarity as expressed at Vatican II.

There are further major theological and ecclesiological issues here that are not acknowledged by the CDF – there are two distinct strands within the Church's theological thinking, as mentioned above – the classicist and the historical consciousness. There is also what is called people of God ecclesiology and Communion ecclesiology. Both were evident at Vatican II. Communion ecclesiology stresses the sacramental, Christological and Eucharistic nature of the Church as the body of Christ. People of God ecclesiology incorporates the historical reality of a pilgrim people (all people including the clerical caste) who fall short of excellence, in need of renewal, conversion and reform. Historical consciousness has room for prophetic call and response. A healthy Church would contain both motifs in balance. However, during the pontificate of John Paul II with Josef Ratzinger as his right hand man, and Benedict XVI's own pontificate, the Communion model was exalted at the expense of the prophetic people of God model. This was felt right through the structure of the Church and, over time, had most impact at parish level.

To ignore or dismiss historical consciousness just because it does not fit into the worldview of the consultor is not acceptable. To judge one method by the propositions of the other is untenable - intellectually, theologically and practically. They are as different as trying to judge the culture and norms of one country by the culture and norms of another (and colonial history has shown how disastrous that is).

This mis-judgement enables the consultor to accuse Seán, unfairly, of calling:

> ...[the] Church's understanding of revelation, human nature and natural law ... into question [and doing this] in order to dismiss the authentic teaching of the Magisterium on the existence of moral absolutes, and finally on the basis of this rejection, specific moral teachings of the Catholic Church are called into question.

This is an appalling accusation. Seán consistently refers to the Church's teaching in his writings. Perhaps the difference is that for him the Church's teaching is that which was renewed at the Second Vatican Council – the teaching that embraced both Communion and people of God models of Church. The very many intelligent Catholics who read *Does Morality Change?* did not interpret the book as dismissing the authentic teaching of the magisterium. Rather, they were comforted and consoled by it. It helped many to "relativise their false absolutes" and give them a renewed enthusiasm for their Church. An enthusiasm, it needs be said, that has been relentlessly beaten down by the Church, both from Rome and within Ireland, in the 22 years since the book's first publication in 1997.

Competence?

Again, showing a serious mis-step in theological competence, the consultor writes above as if there is a single, unambiguous, juridical definition of natural law in the Church. There is not – either inside or outside the Church. This fact is often an eye-opener for the adult student of theology. Before there were any elaborate systems of philosophy, there was the accumulated wisdom of human experience and shared insights. These varied across ethnic groups and were influenced by the exigencies of survival. Over time, this wisdom and experience began to coalesce into accepted systems or codes of behaviour and were accompanied by a rationale for that code. These systems developed in various ways to varying degrees of complexity over time. Ancient Greek philosophy is the system that has been most influential in Christianity in general, and in Catholicism in particular.

There are several current understandings of natural law, most stemming from Thomas Aquinas' definition of humankind as natural beings using our reason to intuit the divine law. This intuition, as we have seen, is not always perfect. Human beings make mistakes and grow in knowledge and understanding – it is natural to our humanity. We learn new things from the advance of science and technology, including the social sciences – new insights that were not possible in previous eras. Given that it is made up of people, the Church too shares in the limitations of the cultures in which it is situated, and should be aware of this. The moral theologian, Bernard Häring, said that the Church should always be open and sensitive to learning and to any new possibility of sharing insights. "She should not be allowed to wallow in outdated formulas; a vision of natural law is genuine if it is dynamic and filled with hope." (*Hope is the Remedy*, p.117)

Often where there is a complaint about the understanding of natural law, the complainant has an overly biological and existentially static understanding of it, usually to the exclusion of all the other aspects that go to make us human.

Natural law in the non-religious sense arises from the human need and ability to discern what is good and bad, and means that we are required to act responsibly. In the faith-sense, it has rather more depth. Natural law is about reflecting on human nature. It reflects on all that makes us human and not just our biology. Human beings seek to understand themselves and the world around them. This includes a questioning at the heart of our moral consciousness – what am I to do? We are responsible for how we live and what we do. As we attempt to understand our experience, often in conversation with others, we come up with different ideas and insights. Out of this searching and conversation questions arise for our judgment and discernment, which test if our understanding is true. This in turn raises further questions for thought and discussion. These questions take us beyond the initial stages of knowing and feeling to the moment of decision and commitment.

> ...It is the law of being open and attentive to our experience, of being intelligent and insightful in our inquiries, of being reasonable and comprehensive in our judgements, of being detached and responsible in our deliberations, of being committed to the good that we discover. If we observe these precepts well, we will arrive at the true and the good. And this is what natural law fundamentally is.
>
> (Harrington, *What Is Morality?* p.104)

Thomas Aquinas also had the wisdom and knowledge to know that in practical matters, the more something is reduced to concrete instances and particular detail, the less clear the answers may be (*Summa Theologica*, I-II, q.94, a.4).

Having had that brief look at natural law, it is relevant here to ask the question: Who was this consultor? As with Seán's accuser, the consultor was also anonymous. Was he a practising theologian? Did he have a track record of teaching and/or publishing? Did he have any pastoral experience? We do not know. Was there more than one consultor? Was a person expert in the field invited to give an opinion?

Further questions on procedure

In the CDF's own *Regulations for Doctrinal Examination* (29th August 1997), Article 4 states that the collaboration of "one or more consultors or other experts in the particular area" may be involved in an investigation. How many people were involved in the examination of Seán's book? Was the opinion offered that of just one person? Again, we do not know – it's all shrouded in secrecy. Yet this person (or persons) stood in anonymous judgement on a man who spent his life working in the light, standing over anything he had to say, and not in the darkness of anonymity and secrecy. Furthermore, Article 10 of *Regulations* states that in the course of an examination, a person is appointed:

> who has the task of illustrating in a spirit of truth the positive aspects of the teaching and the merits of the author, of cooperating in the authentic interpretation of his thought within the overall theological context and of expressing a judgment regarding the influence of the author's opinions.

Was such a person, the *relator pro auctore*, appointed in Seán Fagan's case? There is no named person in the correspondence, so we do not know. And if not, then why not – given that it is part of the examination process? What I *do* know is that there was *never* any reference in *any* of the correspondence available to me that such an advocate was ever appointed to contextualise Seán's work, as laid down by the CDF's own rules. Such an omission only makes sense if there was no *relator pro auctore* or that if a *relator* was appointed, his opinion was of such little consequence it did not merit any reference. Why was it acceptable for the CDF to flout its own rules and procedures?

I believe there is reason to assume that either no *relator pro auctore* was appointed, or that one guaranteed to give the desired result was appointed, and therefore could not fairly present the author's case. It refers to a point I made earlier. There is a fundamental, critical flaw in the *Observations* supplied by the anonymous consultor to the CDF which were presented to Seán, always indirectly, through his religious superior. It is clear the person was operating out of the classicist model of theology, which is propositional and deductive. Seán's theology, deeply influenced by Vatican II, operated within the model of historical consciousness which allows for the contingency of time and culture. It is mostly inductive, but accepts there are fundamental truths to be upheld. This difference in theological perspective is akin to speaking in two different languages. They are fundamentally incompatible, and attempting to judge one by the propositions of the other simply makes no sense. Any competent *relator* would have understood this immediately and suggested that consultors/experts from a historical-consciousness method of theology be invited to submit opinions on Seán's book on the critical issues of method and context. Why, in following the CDF's own rules, was this not done? One suspects that Seán could not be attacked with such ease and with such ferocity if the book was judged by the merits of the method of inquiry used to write it.

Intransigence

We will take a slight detour here and conclude with some of the insights of Yves Congar OP, who suffered greatly at the hands of the CDF for many years. He was ultimately vindicated by being one of the most influential theologians at the Second Vatican Council. His substantial journal of Vatican II (*My Journal of the Council*) is recommended reading because, apart from the factual matters of the Council, one gets some insight into the deep passion Congar had for the Church, while contextualising his writings.

For my purposes here, I draw on the article 'Yves Congar's battle with intransigent conservatism' by Paul Philibert OP, (*Doctrine & Life*, May-June 2012, pp.12-25) as a useful distillation of Congar's worry about intransigence in the Church. Congar believed that the Church "had to be a living organism, as opposed to a church that was merely a museum of past spiritual treasures". In the preparation of the documents for Vatican II, Congar struggled continuously against the forces that wanted no change and who, at times, would use any means available to achieve their aims. Congar identified eight characteristics of this intransigent worldview:

1. It is usually pessimistic. It focuses on original sin, fallen nature and evil in the world. It has a strong tendency to condemn, even if the thing is inoffensive in itself.

2. It rules by imposing its view through the exercise of authority and an appeal to hierarchical powers. It feels no need to justify itself and considers it legitimate to investigate suspect people or doctrines in secret.

3. It cannot cope with the concept of evolution and development of doctrine. To speak of 'experience' suggests relativism.

4. It cannot accept that people might have 'easy access' to the Catholic community – divorced and remarried people having access to the Eucharist for example. "Its inclination is to insist on every jot and tittle of the law, even to maximise the demands of what it means to be Catholic" (p.17). Although, as Philibert points out, there was the "dramatic exception of facilitating Anglicans to enter the Catholic communion as intact diocesan communities..."(ibid. n.4). But of course in that case there was the deep-seated ideological bond of the denial of episcopal ordination to women. Bad enough to have women priests, women bishops were unthinkable.

5. It emphasises dogmatic formulae of what is to be believed rather than any subjective apprehension of faith.

6. Its thinking is deductive, relying on argumentation from premise to conclusion. It does not like the perceived 'messiness' of inductive thinking which takes experience into account. Anything that cannot be neatly defined is seen as relativism. Experience or personal witness is seen as individualism.

7. This mindset emphasises strict authoritarianism. It maximises the authority to be given to any statement from Rome, and lends itself to 'creeping infallibility'. They cannot conceive the truth as a fullness that arises out of a community of believers who, by virtue of their baptism, are filled with the gifts of the Spirit.

   In Congar's words:
   > These people sniff out heresy anywhere they find someone searching seriously for the expression of the truth or in dialogue with contemporary problems.

   (*True and False Reform in the Church, Appendix III*)

8. A particular kind of ecclesiology corresponds to this attitude. It is very positive about the spiritual life, but sees it very much as part of one's personal life. The Church itself is only considered according to the structure of authority, as something exterior to the believing person. Everything is considered as coming from 'on high'. It emphasises "what *was*, what is *given*, what is *commanded*" (*Doctrine & Life*, p.18, emphasis in the original).

It is salutary to note that direct quote from Congar above is from the first edition of his book in French in 1950, *Vraie et Fausse Réforme dans l'Église*. The same attitude has lost none of its fervour in the intervening decades and has reigned supreme in the offices of the CDF. It exists also in the wider Church, and is very visible with the ascendant of the political right. As Congar points out, such a mind-set prefers order to justice because "it is assured of its rectitude from on high through precepts and authority" (*Doctrine & Life*, p.16).

CHAPTER SIX

Punishment

The CDF's attention to Seán waxed and waned from 1998 to July 2004 (but it never interacted directly with him). As mentioned earlier, after the judgement of *Does Morality Change?* in the *Observations* there was a threat that Seán would have to attend at the CDF's offices in Rome to answer the charges in person. However, after some time it was decided in Rome to put the issue back in the hands of the Irish bishops. They were instructed in early 2000, by the CDF, to issue a *Notification* regarding the book. This is, in effect, a warning about the content of book. They were slow to respond to the order of the CDF. They knew the local situation. They knew Seán Fagan. In September 2002 Seán was told, off the record, that he really needn't worry. The bishops were not especially anxious to speak out against him. One imagines, given all the problems of the institutional Church in Ireland at that time with the revelations of clerical child sexual abuse and cover-up by some bishops, disciplining a dedicated priest, who worked solidly and sincerely for the Church (as evidenced by his writings) was not top of their list of priorities.

Does Morality Change? 2.0 - kickback

As mentioned earlier, in 2003 *Does Morality Change?* was reissued in a second edition by The Columba Press because it was still on reading lists in most theological courses within Ireland and the first edition had gone out of print. This was also the year of Seán's Golden Jubilee of ordination and the late Seán O'Boyle saw it as a fitting tribute to him to mark his 50 years of priesthood. As the threat of sanction appeared to have receded, Seán was quite happy to have the book republished. When he sent a copy to his superior general, Fr Jan Hulshof, the reply was affirming and positive. He thanked Seán for the book and copies of various articles by Seán that had been published, which he acknowledged that he found helpful:

> I am certainly not the first to compliment you for the clear and accessible language in which you succeed in explaining quite complicated things....
>
> I wish you every blessing in your teaching ministry. Accompanying theologically people who try to find their way in the midst of many new problems for which the old answers no longer work is a great service.
>
> (*SF Dossier/JH/SF/03-03*)

There was no reason for Seán to be particularly concerned about this new edition of *Does Morality Change?* especially as it had a shorter print run than his previous books and the Vatican inquiry appeared to have gone into abeyance.

However, the anonymous accuser was on point because, without much delay, the CDF not only became aware of its existence, but had written to the Irish bishops by early September 2003 with an official *Notification* against the book. In early 2004, Cardinal Josef Ratzinger, Prefect of the CDF, wrote to the Irish Bishops through Cardinal Seán Brady and personally demanded that the Irish Episcopal Conference issue a statement about *Does Morality Change?*. He said the publication of the 2003 edition:

> ...cannot be interpreted as anything other than confirmation of the lack of good faith on the part of the author... It

is an injustice which calls for the response of the Bishops' Conference of Ireland.

(*SF Dossier*/JR/SB/03-1)

Of all the events or activities happening in the Irish Church in the early decades of the millennium, highlighting the re-print of what had been a very well-received book as an "injustice" displays an unacceptable level of ignorance about the state of the Church in Ireland at the time. This ignorance is further reinforced by other comments in Cardinal Ratzinger's letter. The reason the CDF wanted the Irish bishops to issue a *Notification* against *Does Morality Change?* was "...in order to protect the faith of the Catholic people in Ireland and elsewhere from its manifestly harmful contents". If this is a serious understanding in the Vatican of what constituted an 'injustice', comment is superfluous.

Episcopal autonomy

That the head of a Vatican department could demand that a national bishops' conference act on a particular issue, raises significant issues about the authority of the bishop in his diocese. Tradition is a very important part of the Church's life. What is not found directly in scripture, is understood to be found in the tradition of the Church (which is considered to be the authentic interpretation of scripture, and logically secondary to it) under the guidance of the Holy Spirit. The autonomy of a bishop in his diocese has a long tradition in the Church. But it would seem this can either be invoked or ignored, depending on the circumstances. The view of the autonomy of the bishop's role was quite different in Malawi in the late 1980s. Irishman, Fr John Roche, SPS, a missionary priest in Malawi, was called to Rome and told he was the preferred nominee to take over the running of the Diocese of Mzuzu as Apostolic Administrator (as bishop, but without the official title). Given that John's own expressed preference was for an indigenous candidate to be nominated, he was concerned about what authority he might have in the role, especially if priests resented his appointment. He was told very clearly and unambiguously that he would be "a little pope in your own diocese".

When the Irish bishops exercised their legitimate right, as individual leaders collegially acting, not to openly sanction Seán Fagan in 2000, they were operating out of a long tradition of autonomy that was rightfully theirs. However, this autonomy was trampled upon with the irate demand from Cardinal Josef Ratzinger in early 2004. In his letter Cardinal Ratzinger spoke of the "dialogue between this Congregation and Father Fagan, prior to the involvement of the Irish Episcopal Conference" that was made known to them [the Irish bishops] in early 2000, and "...not only were the details of this dialogue communicated, but the relevant documentation... was provided". This information is wholly misleading. It is untrue that there was 'dialogue' between the CDF and Seán Fagan. Seán was never directly contacted by any person in the CDF, either in writing or in person. The only contact was with Seán's religious superior, the head of the Marist congregation. It was manifestly untrue, therefore, to state that "the details of this dialogue..." were communicated to the Irish bishops, because there was no dialogue with Seán, not ever, during the whole process.

As mentioned above, the autonomy of the bishops seems to be a rather fluid concept depending on the requirements of the Vatican central government. When they want to keep a distance – it is being "a little pope in your own diocese" but when they want action they have no compunction about demanding compliance. In this case, the CDF gave the Irish bishops an ultimatum to issue a *Notification* against *Does Morality Change?* before the end of May 2004. The Irish Bishops' Conference then capitulated and issued a statement which eventually appeared on its website, in a very circumspect way, in July 2004.

Reactions

Some people would have been quite pleased to see this *Notification* published. For example, Dr Gerard Casey, then a lecturer in philosophy in UCD "...welcomed the Irish bishops' response to a book they say is 'in error'". According to *The Irish Catholic* newspaper, Dr Casey had previously called on the bishops to respond to the book *Does Morality Change?* given what he called its contradictory message on natural law. He is quoted as saying: "Opposing views can be acceptable to the Church within the parameters of Church teaching". The particular definition of natural law Dr Casey had in mind is not stated, nor is his concept of the 'Church' that offers Church teaching – white, male, clerical and Eurocentric? These are important clarifications. Dr Casey told *The Irish Catholic* in August 2004 that Fr Seán Fagan "should now reflect on his position".

On the other hand, one of Ireland's leading theologians, Fr Gabriel Daly, OSA, said he was "deeply shamed and disappointed" by the capitulation of the Irish bishops to the CDF. He further added: "The authorities in the Church are getting worse all the time. I would love to see the bishops stand up to Rome in matters of this sort. I regret the lack of openness, transparency and accountability on their part." (*Irish Independent*, 04.08.04, p.9)

One supportive and particularly sensitive letter arrived, quite unexpectedly, from a man in Yorkshire who said:

> I write to offer some solidarity with you and your writings. ...If I write to you, it is because from my days at Louvain a long time ago, I saw the hurt that was caused to fine scholars... from a Roman attack on their work. Intellectually it is easy enough to disregard criticism that has little scholarship behind it. But there is often a wound that goes unexpectedly deep and does not readily heal, partly because there are few attacks from within a family that do not cause hurt, and partly

because one is pained for a Church that fails to live up to its mission of unrelenting search for truth.

... And underlying again the apparently theoretical apparatus of Vatican thinking is a morbid concern with rejecting contraception that is poisoning a great part of the contemporary moral teaching, and even effort, of the Church.

... Finally, I regret that the bishops of my country of origin did not have more courage than they have shown. Yet it is fair to say that they have in a covert way distanced themselves as much from the 'condemnation' as they dared within our present centralising structures. Still it is sad when bishops become proconsular officials of an imperial regime than representative guardians of their own communities.

This letter struck a particular chord with Seán, especially the words: "But there is often a wound that goes unexpectedly deep and does not readily heal, partly because there are few attacks from within a family that do not cause hurt...." This is a truth that those who were close to Seán in his years of persecution could see writ large in his life.

The Irish bishops' statement was entitled 'Recent developments in moral theology and their implications for the Church and Society.' There are 11 short sections to the document. Sections 1-7 speak about morality in general, leading to acknowledgment of the renewal of moral theology after Vatican II. A renewal that was necessary "to overcome the excessive, not to say rigorist legalism of the dominant moral theology before the Council, with its concentration on sin". In section 8 we get to the specifics:

The renewal of moral theology inevitably brought about a number of developments, which in the attempt to find a better articulation of the fundamental principles within the context of contemporary culture, can only be described inadequate, or, indeed erroneous, as not being in harmony with the Church's teaching or the wisdom of humanity. One such attempt to articulate a renewed fundamental moral theology is that found in the book *Does Morality Change?* by Father Seán Fagan, S.M. (Dublin: Gill & Macmillan; Collegeville: The Liturgical Press, 1997). The value of making such an attempt is to be recognised. However, this book contains a number of errors common to similar attempts at renewal (§8).

These errors, as listed, are:

(a) The denial of the binding force of the magisterium on conscience

(b) The uncritical acceptance of the tendency to 'substitute a dynamic and more evolutionary concept of nature for a static one'

(c) The effective rejection of the Church's understanding of natural law

(d) The explicit denial of moral absolutes, specifically those concrete acts which are intrinsically wrong

(e) The promotion of a false understanding of conscience

Veritatis splendor

Here is where we come to the nub of the problem. In order to address such 'errors' as listed above and which are attributed to the renewal in moral theology since Vatican II, John Paul II issued an encyclical called *Veritatis Splendor* in 1993. This encyclical was a shock to many in the community of moral theologians. Bernard Häring, probably the most important reforming moral theologian of the 20th Century, had what he called "seizures of the brain" several hours after reading it. He was 80 years old at the time and still working in moral theology. He wrote in *The Tablet* in 1993:

> *Veritatis Splendor* contains many beautiful things. But almost all real splendour is lost when it becomes evident that the whole document is directed above all towards one goal: to endorse total assent and submissions to all utterances of the Pope, and above all on one crucial point: that the use of any artificial means for regulating birth is intrinsically evil and sinful, without exception, even in circumstances where contraception would be the lesser evil.
>
> The Pope is confident that he has a binding duty to proclaim his teachings with no calculation whatsoever about the foreseeable practical consequences for the people concerned and for the whole Church. He would consider such considerations unlawful and dangerous, because they take into account a weighing of values. Whatever the risk, whatever the danger, he believes his insights brook no dissent, but can be met only with obedience.
>
> ...As a moral theologian, John Paul I [Albino Luciani] shared fully the convictions of the vast majority of moral theologians of the past and the present that it is unlawful and possibly a great injustice to impose on people heavy burdens in the name of God unless it is fully clear that it this is really God's will.
>
> In *Veritatis Splendor* John Paul II [Karol Wojtyla] makes no secret that he has for a number of years felt driven to write an encyclical to bring theologians into line with his teaching on sexual morals, particularly on contraception.
>
> ...Its words will press hard on the consciences of all concerned, though clearly the Pope and his special advisor do not

have a proper picture of what moral theology today is like. Very grave insinuations are made. What moral theologian of good reputation in the Church would recognise himself in the picture which *Veritatis Splendor* draws?

(The Tablet, 23.10.93, pp.1378-79)

Häring goes on to point out that the vast majority of married people have made up their own minds with regard to contraception. He also acknowledges that "most moral theologians, probably, are of the same mind". He then says:

Let us ask our Pope: are you sure your confidence in your supreme human, professional and religious competence in matters of moral theology and particularly sexual ethics is truly justified?

Speaking about contraception, Häring says that this is a matter of:

...what we call the natural law written deep in the hearts of men and women, and therefore we must and can find a fruitful approach which is appropriate. Since natural law is "open to the eyes of reason" we should reason together gently and patiently as we consider the case "on either side" (Rom 2:12,16). The hierarchical constitution of the Church cannot in the least contradict or disallow this approach in any matter which concerns the law written in our hearts and calling for a response from our consciences.

This is from a man who describes himself in questions of sexual morality, "as pastorally kind but theologically rather conservative". Reading any of Häring's autobiographical material, it is obvious that he was very deferential to hierarchical structure of the Church. He was always willing to give the benefit of the doubt to Church teaching, and was quite reserved in his opinions where he had not come to a clear judgment. But when he had, such as in the matter of birth control, he was quite strong in standing up for what he believed. He was horrified by the implications of *Veritatis Splendor* for the practice of moral theology. Theological competence mattered to Häring. Authority by itself did not imply competence. Therefore, when someone of his stature says:

> Away with all distrust in our Church! Away with all attitudes, mentalities and structures that promote it! We should let the Pope know that we are wounded by the many signs of his rooted distrust, and discouraged by the manifold structures of distrust which he has allowed to be established. We need him to soften towards us, we, the whole Church needs it. Our witness to the world needs it. The urgent call to ecumenism needs it.

It ought to be a clarion call to sit up and take notice. The highly regarded British moral theologian Kevin T. Kelly met Häring on three occasions. He said of their second meeting:

> I have a most vivid memory of concelebrating Mass with him... along with two other priests. We were the only ones with him in this small chapel. I had the impression of sharing in the Eucharistic celebration of a saint. He was not pious in any trivial sense. Perhaps I can best express what I felt by saying the Eucharist that morning seemed to express the wonder of his being. His whole being was Eucharistic – deeply appreciative of the goodness of life and people and overflowing with gratitude to God.

> (*50 Years of Receiving Vatican II*, p.226)

It is worth noting that Härings's *cri-de-coeur* was made in 1993, four years before the publication of *Does Morality Change?*. Not only was the plea by the most eminent moral theologian of the day ignored, but *Veritatis Splendor* was the yardstick by which all moral theology writings, including *Does Morality Change?* were subsequently judged. Of the 11 pages of the *Observations* by the anonymous consultor, three were directly related to the encyclical. This is also borne out in the Irish bishops' statement; they refer to *Veritatis Splendor* specifically in their admonishment of Seán.

The concern about *Veritatis Splendor* is very important in this case, and for anyone who wishes to read further into the theology of the document, the essays in the book *The Splendour of Accuracy* edited by Joseph A. Selling and Jan Jans, is a very good starting point and is an excellent critique. The critique on the use of scripture in *Veritatis Splendor* is particularly interesting, especially on the issue of "intrinsically evil acts" as listed in the *Observations* and in the demand of the CDF as to the content of the statement they wanted Seán to issue. Gareth Moore OP offers a detailed discussion on the use of scripture in *Veritatis Splendor* and the argumentation drawn from it. He concludes:

> Most of the scriptural work is done in chapter one [of *Veritatis Splendor*]. If I am correct in my assessment of the argumentation here, its scriptural basis is questionable and flawed in more than one way. Pope John Paul has performed an important service in stressing again that scripture is the fundamental source of Christian morality; but the particular way in which he has used that source is imperfect. It is at best a partial view of the moral teaching of scripture, and the pope's specific concerns – the inadequacies of certain modern moral theories – are not reflected in scripture. This is not, of course, to say that those concerns are not justified; but the particular justification sought for them in scripture is not to be found. (p.97)

When issued in 2004, the Irish bishops' statement appeased the CDF for there were no more threats from that quarter towards Seán Fagan and matters settled for a few years. Although as Seán pointed out in 2004: "My weak human nature was tempted to think that if only I had been a paedophile I might get better treatment" (*SF Dossier/SF/JH/04-02*).

Friends of Seán, disgusted at the Irish bishops' caving in to Curial pressure, wanted to honour him and show appreciation for his huge contribution to the Church in Ireland. A volume of essays, *Quench Not The Spirit*, was published by The Columba Press in 2005, edited by Dr David Smith MSC and myself. In the spirit of Seán's pastoral imperative, his was not a formal academic festschrift but a more general anthology of Church-related essays. The launch of the book in May 2005 was a marvellous occasion. The affirmation of the very large crowd of people who attended gave Seán a much needed morale boost at a time when it was sorely lacking from those who should have been grateful for Seán's representation of what it was to be Church. But the calm was relatively short-lived.

CHAPTER SEVEN

Endgame

In 2008 the CDF reacted severely, and out of all proportion, to the content of a letter sent by Seán to Letters to the Editor page of *The Irish Times* about the shortage of priests, published on 10th July, 2008. This letter included a tangential opinion on the ordination of women and acceptance of married priests in the Church. There was nothing unusual about this as the same opinion has been voiced many times, by many other people over the years. A photocopy of this letter was sent to the CDF in Rome within two weeks of its publication. As can be seen below, the issue under discussion in the newspaper was not the ordination of women, as such, it was about the shortage of priests around the world.

> Madam, - Shane Halpin's letter of July 8th and David Rice's excellent report on the lesson we might learn from the Catholic Church in France (*Rite and Reason*, same date) could be a wake-up call for Ireland.
>
> Forty years after the Second Vatican Council our church here is still very much a clerical church. Before describing how the church was hierarchically organised, that council (the highest teaching authority in the church) stressed that the essential definition of the church was 'the People of God'.
>
> Because of our clerical history in Ireland, even the laity still subconsciously think of the church in terms of bishops and priests. A little bit of theology and history might shake us

free of that straitjacket to enable us to see some more radical solutions to current problems. 'Radical' is used here in its sense of 'going back to our roots' as a Christian church.

The Vatican recently ordered bishops around the world to appoint a priest to organise special prayer meetings and adoration of the Blessed Sacrament to pray for vocations. We have been praying for decades for more priests in Latin America and now in our home countries, but we fail to see that perhaps God has already answered our prayers: that God is not interested in 'more of the same'. God is asking us to use our God-given reason and common sense to search for new answers.

There is no need to close or sell the church building. We could ordain a working man or woman or a recently retired person to celebrate the Eucharist and bring the sacraments to the sick and dying. Everything else can be taken care of by a well organised Christian community of lay people with their various gifts, as they are doing brilliantly in France. The 'official' Church may not be ready yet for married priests and women priests, but they will come in God's good time.

For the first hundred years after the death of Jesus, Christianity was not recognised as a religion and there were no churches. The Eucharist was celebrated in private houses and the leader was somebody appointed by an apostle or a man elected by the community. More often the leader of the celebration would be the owners of the house, who could be a married couple or a rich widow. Only later was the leader prayed over by the laying on of hands, and only very slowly did our present notion of priesthood develop.

Many people imagine that at the Last Supper Jesus ordained the apostles as priests, giving them everything except Roman collars. But in fact there is nothing in the gospels to show that Jesus consciously founded the Church, or even a church. Nor did he ever ordain anyone a priest in the modern sense, or even think of a cultic priesthood.

Inspired by the early history of our Christian communities and the division of ministries, we should be free to devise a healthy and human re-organisation that could revitalise our parishes. - Yours, etc,

Fr Seán Fagan, Lr Leeson St., Dublin 2.

The then superior general of the Marists, Fr Jan Hulshof, was contacted by the CDF. I do not have access to that communication, but from other communications that followed that I have seen, it is clear that its purpose was to insist that Seán withdraw his comment regarding women's ordination. Seán refers to this in correspondence with Fr John Hannan, a former student of Seán's who later succeeded Fr Hulshof as superior general of the Society of Mary in 2009. In his letter Seán says Fr Hulshof "was *ordered* to *command* me to publicly retract my reference to ordaining women..." [emphasis in original] (*SF Dossier/JH/SF/*10-2). Not only that, but he was to cease making any statements in the future that were at variance with the CDF's interpretation of Church teaching. As can be seen from the full text above, this letter was not about women's ordination *per se,* nor was it actively making a case for it. Yet, it set off a reaction within the CDF that was utterly out of proportion to the purpose and intent of the letter.

This instruction regarding Seán's letter to *The Irish Times* went through the usual channels of communication used by the CDF so that it was not Seán they contacted, but his superior general, Fr Jan Hulshof. Fr Hulshof then passed on the instruction to Seán's immediate superior, Fr John Hannan, Marist Provincial in Europe at the time. Fr Hannan was tasked with telling Seán in September 2008 that because of John Paul II's apostolic letter *Ordinatio Sacerdotalis*

(1994) on the reservation of priestly ordination to men only, Seán's aside on the possibility of women priests potentially put him in the position of being excommunicated. It was seen as expressing an opinion that was contrary to the definitive doctrine of the Church – that women cannot be ordained. That would be seen as a refusal of the truth of that Catholic doctrine, therefore, he would no longer be in communion with the Catholic Church. Despite the knowledge that there were likely to be sanctions placed upon him, Seán replied to his religious superiors that he could not in conscience, make the statement required by the CDF, as "it would portray the Church as on a par with Communist China..." By this he meant Communism under Mao Tse Tung. In November 2008 in communication with Fr John Hannan, he said:

> To go through some 'procedure' to keep the Vatican happy would be against the old classical moral theology about *cooperatio in malo* [co-operation with evil]. I am in no way concerned about my own reputation, but I love the Church too much to harm it in this way.
>
> (*SF Dossier/SF/JH/08-07*)

Instead of a retraction of the letter, Seán undertook to cease making any public statements on Church matters. He was true to his word and turned down five invitations from Irish radio and television stations and one from the BBC in Belfast. He hoped his self-imposed silence would pacify the CDF.

Creeping infallibility

There are some points to be noted here. Firstly, the issue of women's ordination began in a very low-key way in the late 1960s, early 1970s. It was beginning to find some momentum in the late 1980s, and by the early 1990s was starting to gain some traction. Then, quite suddenly, John Paul II issued *Ordinatio Sacerdotalis* in 1994, saying not only could women not be ordained, but the topic could not even be discussed. Without full academic research and detailed discussion, the issue was peremptorily closed down.

Secondly, a mark of John Paul II's pontificate, with Cardinal Ratzinger as head of the CDF, is what is called 'creeping infallibility.' If something was declared 'definitively to be held,' it really could not be discussed or disputed openly – not even in the academic environment. This 'creeping infallibility' was enhanced and given official stamp by a document called *Ad Tuendam Fidem* issued in May 1998. This document caused great concern in the theological community because of the implications for doctrinal development. Thirdly, the CDF was obviously quite exercised by the book *Does Morality Change?*, yet they decided not to call Seán to a tribunal in Rome on foot of their concerns, but left it to the Irish bishops (with some severe prodding). That a letter that mentions women's ordination simply as an aside could cause such a reaction is quite astounding. It certainly contextualises Mary McAleese's comments about the misogynistic structure of the Church at the Voices of Faith conference, *Why Women Matter*, on 8th March, 2018.

The autocratic pontificate of John Paul II, together with the assistance of Cardinal Josef Ratzinger, head of the CDF, centralised in the Vatican much of the rights and duties that rightfully belonged to the bishops, with whom he was supposed to be acting collegially. This was clearly seen in various synods that happened through the 1980s where the input of the world's bishops to what were meant to be collegial gatherings became almost irrelevant to the eventual outcome. They were really present to do little more than rubber stamp the decisions made by John Paul II with the advice of those closest to him. A significant characteristic of this autocracy was the expectation that when he issued a teaching document it was to be accepted fully, without question. This is where the problem for Seán Fagan and many other moral theologians lay. Can a teaching be obeyed? In 1999 in a letter to the editor of *Céide*, an excellent, if short-lived bi-monthly magazine, published in the West of Ireland, Seán stated:

> ...there is a wider confusion with regard to Church teaching that is crying out for clarification. Many official teaching documents give the impression that truth can be decreed and imposed, whereas in fact it can only be discovered and shared. It is a nonsense to ask *Do you obey the Church's teaching in this particular matter?* This is a category mistake, using obedience outside of its proper category of meaning. Obedience is the response to a command, not to teaching. Good teachers never ask students if they *obey* what has been taught, but would be concerned to know whether they understand and are convinced by it, and in that sense, accept it. Too often Aristotle's basic principle is forgotten that no teaching takes place until someone has been taught.
>
> (*Céide*, Jan-Feb 1999), [emphasis in the original]

What Happened to Sin? (Book three)

While the CDF was still very exercised by what was little more than an aside in the letter to *The Irish Times* in July 2008, and demanding a retraction, Seán's most recent publication *What Happened to Sin?* (a revision of his highly-acclaimed 1977 book *Has Sin Changed?*) caused an ever-increasing negative reaction from the CDF. A new instruction had been issued by the CDF in 1992 requiring that permission had to be sought from the major religious superior for permission to have a book published. None of the fellow theologians Seán contacted, at home and abroad, were aware of this new type of imprimatur and all had written extensively, including in the time since 1992, without it. Seán examined over 20 books from his shelves, published by either Veritas or The Columba Press over the previous ten years, none of which had this imprimatur. However, it has to be said that this requirement was brought to Seán's attention by his Regional Superior after the 2003 reprint of *Does Morality Change?* Unfortunately, by Seán's own admission, he had forgotten about the requirement, as it had not been an issue for him before then, in anything he had published.

Seán undertook the rewrite of his original book *Has Sin Changed?* in August 2005, following the very positive reaction to *Quench not the Spirit*, the book of essays published in his honour. This anthology of essays reminded many people of his ground-breaking *Has Sin Changed?* and the positive influence it had in their lives in the late 1970s and early 1980s. Some of Seán's UK friends encouraged him to have it re-published, but he wanted to do a re-write, incorporating inclusive language and to include the scandal of clerical child sexual abuse.

What Happened to Sin? was already fully through the publication process by the time the CDF reacted to the letter in *The Irish Times*, and was published in late October 2008. This caused worry and concern for the Marist leadership at the time, given the pressure they were already under because of the July letter the CDF wanted retracted. One cannot but feel a certain sympathy on a human level for the two men most closely involved - the superior general and the provincial for Europe. They both knew Seán and knew his commitment both to his Marist family and to the Catholic Church. Seán also had concern for them and was sorry that he was the cause of difficulty for them, especially for his provincial Fr John Hannan, for whom he had particular regard. He found the emotional dilemma difficult. However, for Seán there was a greater truth at stake – reaching out to God's people under the gospel mandate to help lift the burdens laid upon them, and the matter of freedom of conscience. So he refused to issue a retraction as a matter of conscience, but also undertook a self-imposed vow of silence to protect the Marist leadership from the attentions of the CDF. However, this was not without suffering. In 2008, following a meeting in Dublin about his situation, he wrote to his provincial about achieving a workable solution to the CDF's demand:

> Of course I am in the dark, reminding me of an aspect of my situation not realised by those who are not victims of the CDF, namely made to feel that I am a mentally defective teenager with others writing about me to each other over my head and not involving me, but this is normal procedure for the Vatican.

> (*SF Dossier/SF/JH/08-10*)

A particular concern for Seán resulting from internal meetings at this time was a suggestion that the Marists would buy up all copies of *What Happened to Sin?*. Seán was horrified at the proposal. For him this equated with the medieval book burnings sanctioned by Church leaders, and other book burnings that happened in totalitarian states. This was not just because it was his own book – he was equally horrified back in the 1990s when Sr Lavinia Byrne's book *Woman at the Altar* was withdrawn from circulation (many believe it was pulped). It was written and had gone through the process of publication prior to John Paul II's apostolic letter *Ordinatio Sacardotalis* in 1994. Byrne, in her effort to be true and fair, insisted that *Ordinatio Sacerdotalis* be included as an appendix to her book, despite the fact this caused significant logistical problems for her publisher. But her fairness and integrity were not considered good enough; her book had to be withdrawn. As mentioned, Seán was horrified at the parallels between this action and public medieval book burnings. He spoke of 'book burning' when referring to the possibility of the removal of his book from public access. He said in a letter to the Provincial in late 2008:

The suggestion that the Marist province should buy and destroy the unsold copies of the *Sin* book does not come from the CDF and I would prefer that it not be mentioned (or offered) to the CDF. Should this become public I believe that my vow of obedience and promise of silence would not include this. Like so many thousands of committed Catholics around the world, I am ashamed of the procedures of the CDF, but if the book burning were to go ahead I would also be ashamed of the Marist Congregation, not only for reverting to this medieval practice, but more so for wasting a huge amount of money which should go to the poor or our needy missions around the world. This makes a travesty of true religion. I would not want to be part of a deception and cover it up, and force the publisher to tell lies about what happened.

Since the book was published I have been inundated by emails and phone calls from around the world enthusiastically congratulating me on the book. [This may be from Marist communities, as Seán names two confrères as examples, the context is not clear] ... The word most frequently used in these letters to describe the book is 'compassion', which so many Catholics find lacking in our Church today, especially gay and lesbian people and the hundreds of thousands of Catholics who have all the obligations of Catholicism but are refused a share of the Lord's table because of canon law [a reference to divorced and remarried Catholics]. ...

Only this morning I had several phone calls from people who contrasted the huge fuss over my book and the episcopal support (possibly prompted by the Vatican) for bishop John Magee in spite of most of the Irish media clamouring for him to resign for his failure to protect children from paedophile priests whom he did not supervise. [It was another 18 months before John Magee, then bishop of Cloyne, resigned].

(SF Dossier/SF/JH/08-10)

At the time of this letter to *The Irish Times*, there was a general concern among religious about negative publicity for the Church in Ireland. This was just prior to the release of the report on clerical sexual abuse in the Dublin archdiocese. Seán did not personally subscribe to the 'let's not bring shame on the Church' approach. His attitude was always 'admit, accept, adjust'. This meant facing up to your actions (or inactions) and accepting the consequences, learning something from the process, then moving on with a changed attitude and behaviour. Nevertheless, he was willing to stand back because he knew the intensity of the media storm that was in store for the Church following the publication of the *Murphy Report* into clerical sexual abuse in the Dublin archdiocese. Therefore, to be helpful to his religious leaders, and to give them something to show to the CDF, he agreed to the text that was to be submitted to the CDF by the Marist leadership on his punishment, in which it was made clear that Seán undertook a promise of silence with regard to his writing and broadcasting.

There was a further matter here with regard to the publication of *What Happened to Sin?*. It was removed from public access without there being any discussion on its merit. Given that it was an update of Seán's very highly regarded *Has Sin Changed?*, one might have hoped, at a minimum, it would at least be properly examined before it was effectively censored, without due process, by its removal from the bookshops.

Response to Ryan Report

Following publication of the Report by the Commission to Inquire into Child Abuse in Institutions in Ireland (*The Ryan Report*), Seán O'Boyle of

The Columba Press commissioned Fr Tony Flannery to write a response to it. Tony readily agreed, understanding the importance of this shocking report both for Irish society in general and the Church in particular. As he considered the project, Tony decided that a broad range of voices was needed, including some not ordinarily heard. The anthology *Responding to the Ryan Report* was the result, published in 2009.

Seán's chapter, Chapter 1: 'The Abuse and our Bad Theology', gave a background to the poor theology around sexual development and maturity. He pointed out that "Official church teaching today seldom acknowledges the harm done by its centuries-long negative understanding of sexuality" (p.15). He then set out the Church's background of its pessimistic approach to sexuality. There is nothing spectacular in what he says, nor are there any shocking revelations that had not been known up to then, but typically, Seán does not pull his punches. He quotes from *Love and Responsibility* by Karol Wojtyla, published in Polish in 1960. It was published in English in 1981 by Collins & Sons (now HarperCollins), when he was Pope John Paul II. When speaking on sexual intercourse, John Paul II says:

> ...it is the very nature of the act that the man plays the active role and takes the initiative, whilst the woman is a comparatively passive partner, whose function it is to accept and experience. For the purpose of the sexual act it is enough for her to be passive and unresisting, so much so that it can even take place without her volition, while she is in a state in which she has no awareness at all of what is happening, for instance when she is asleep or unconscious.
>
> (p.271 – a new translation was published in 2013 by Ignatius Press)

Of this, Seán asks: "Can this be Catholic Church teaching? It sounds like rape." (p.22) Not an unreasonable question. Not an unreasonable answer.

Seán had no worries about contributing to the *Ryan Report* anthology. There wasn't a whisper of women's ordination in his piece, not even in the short section he had on the Church's anti-feminist attitude. There was nothing about homosexuality which was, with women's ordination, another flash-point for reprisal from Rome. In fact, there was nothing in the chapter that wasn't already in the public domain, from the many writings Seán had published over 50 years of his ministry and from the writings of many others over the same period. He saw his chapter as contributing to the understanding of the problem from a historical perspective. There was nothing discussed that in any way could have affected someone's Catholic faith. He did not perceive this as in any way contrary to his promise to Fr Hannan not to write or broadcast – there was nothing new in it. As he said in an email to his regional leader:

> I have no scruples about doing the chapter of the book. Most clergy do not seem interested and I have not met any of them who have actually read the Ryan report. I would say the main benefit of the chapter is the wider context of the problem...
>
> (*SF Dossier/SF/DC/09-1*)

Of any issue in the Church on which Seán was utterly uncompromising, it was the scandal of clerical child sexual abuse and its tragic consequences for the abused children and minors and their families. He was equally scathing of the cover-up by bishops. It was not surprising then, that if he were to put his head above the parapet about anything it would be on this issue. Because of the availability of all the information in the chapter in other sources, he did not see there could be a problem contributing to the volume – it was historical information already in the public domain. He was invited on to the Vincent Browne programme on RTÉ to discuss *Response to the Ryan Report* but refused because of his promise not to broadcast. The religious affairs correspondent for *The Irish Times*, Patsy McGarry had a telephone conversation with Seán following publication of *Response to the Ryan Report* and quoted him in his article. Again, as it was historical information, Seán had no problem giving background to the journalist. His comment was reported to Rome in less than a week after its publication in the newspaper.

Another condemnation

Without much delay the CDF issued another condemnation of Seán to the Marist religious superior on foot of *Response to the Ryan Report*. This happened much sooner than when the book might be expected to be on sale in Rome (if that were even likely). Whoever the Vatican's spy was in Ireland, he (or possibly she) was working assiduously to keep them informed about Seán Fagan in particular. It is difficult to avoid the conclusion that there was a personal vendetta against him either by an individual cleric or theologian, or a small lay group with a particular agenda. Perhaps it was someone Seán had got the better of during a public discussion or in a Letter to the Editor exchange of a newspaper. I know from many conversations with Seán that he strongly suspected a senior Irish bishop, but he could never know for sure. Some other friends of Seán are quite convinced that it was another Irish theologian who was totally at odds with Seán's compassionate 'people first' pastoral care. Who knows? But there is something deeply repellent about the whole tittle-tattling process so assiduously attended to by some. One could say it was juvenile behaviour, but for its very serious consequences.

CHAPTER EIGHT

Confrontation

On 18th January, 2010, the senior Marist leaders were called to a meeting with Cardinal William Levada, Prefect of the CDF, who was accompanied by Msgr Charles Brown (later Papal Nuncio to Ireland) on the matter of the book *What Happened to Sin?*. At this meeting Cardinal Levada voiced the "extreme concerns" of the CDF at Seán's writings, which they considered contrary to the teaching of the Catholic Church. The Marist leadership attempted to explain the situation of the Church in Ireland and the problems it had, and to make clear that Seán's health was not good (during the years of the CDF's attentions, Seán had many stress-related illnesses and several falls). But all to no avail. In fact, they implied that the Marist leadership were "colluding" with Seán in his "disobedience" (PC 25.01.2010). Furthermore, Fr Hannan was told that if he did not sanction Seán he would be dismissed from his role as superior general and replaced with someone more compliant, who would. This was an appalling threat. Fr John Hannan was freely and fairly elected by the members of the Society of Mary to be their leader for the next eight years. This was an extremely difficult case for him to have to deal with when he was not even six months in the role. The aggressive and bullying tactics of Cardinal Levada were breath-taking in their arrogance. He did not have the authority to dismiss Fr Hannan but seemed wholly ignorant of that fact.

At this meeting of 18th January, it was made clear that Cardinal Levada wanted a penalty imposed on Seán that, if not adhered to by him, would result in the ultimate sanction of his dismissal from priesthood and the Marist family (*SF Dossier /JH/SF/*10-3). It was also clear that the dossier compiled and in the possession of CDF was not the work of a crank, but "the careful compilation of key writings and statements judged to be harmful to the Church's moral teaching". There can be no doubt that the case against Seán Fagan was the result of a methodical, careful and focused pursuit by person or persons unknown with what would seem a determined purpose to silence him.

The message from the CDF was very clear – they, and only they, had the final say on what constituted correct Catholic doctrine. The matter of their competence did not enter the discussion. The reality of the *sensus fidelium* did not enter the discussion either. (The *sensus fidelium* is the instinct or sense of the faithful as it is lived and applied in the Church). The competence of theologians and scripture scholars around the world in their various disciplines did not enter the discussion. The magisterium has come to be equated with the teaching office of the Church and effectively, in recent decades, this means the Pope and the Prefect of the Congregation for the Doctrine of the Faith. In fact, the teaching office of the Church has three distinct authorities: the *sensus fidelium*, theology and the magisterium. All three authorities held in a creative balance benefit the Church, strike down one or two of these authorities, as has happened in the past 40 years, and there is an unbalanced authority that leads to untrammelled abuses of procedure and due process, because it has no corrective.

Cardinal Levada's record

Given Cardinal Levada's insistence on his authority, as Prefect of the CDF, to define and guard Catholic doctrine and mete out punishment on foot of that, it is worth looking a little at his history and competence and, therefore, at his authority as a senior Church leader.

Cardinal Levada had his problems in the Dioceses of Portland and San Francisco prior to his promotion to Rome as head of the CDF. His record on shielding clerical child abusers is shameful. His most notable case was the dismissal of Fr John Conley in San Francisco. Fr Conley made complaints against a fellow priest, Fr James Aylward for abusive advances on a teenage boy. William Levada ordered Conley to stop making public accusations against another cleric, but Conley persisted and reported the incident to the police in 1997. The abuser, Aylward, was quietly moved to another parish, while Conley, the whistleblower, was suspended from priestly ministry. Of course, the archdiocese claimed that Fr Conley was suspended for other reasons than his efforts to have an abuser brought to account.

However, it was discovered that Aylward later settled a lawsuit against him by a young man. And furthermore, the archdiocese paid out $75,000 to Aylward for the settlement. Fr Conley brought a civil action against the diocese for his unfair dismissal. He won both a financial settlement and more importantly, an acknowledgment from the archdiocese that he had done the right thing reporting the incident to the police. This acknowledgment was all the more powerful because Levada had testified that he would not have reported the incident to the police. It helped that Conley was a former assistant U.S. attorney and so he was well aware of his rights and how to pursue them.

Even though Archbishop Levada set up an independent review board in 2002 to examine personnel files of abusive priests, the chairman, psychologist James Jenkins, grew suspicious when Levada would not release the names of priests under scrutiny. A canon lawyer, Fr Greg Ingels, who helped set up the review board and who wrote a guide-book for bishops on the handling of abuse cases, was indicted in 2003 for abusive behaviour with a 15-year-old boy in the 1970s. Archbishop Levada knew of these allegations since 1996 but never made the board aware of the fact. Mr Jenkins resigned as chairman of the review board, accusing Levada of "an elaborate public relations scheme".

Perhaps the most illustrative example of Cardinal Levada's attitude to priests who deserve praise and those who deserve punishment is the case of Bishop Ziemann of Santa Rosa diocese. Ziemann was accused in 2002 and 2004 of historical sexual abuse of minors in a grade school/high school, and a minor seminary. He was also accused of coercing a priest in the diocese, Fr Jorge Hume Salas, into having regular sex with him between 1996 and 1998. He denied the coercion, saying it was consensual, but the priest disputes this. The priest had been removed from a parish for stealing. He said Ziemann coerced him into regular sex in exchange for not revealing the true reason he had been moved from his parish. (Hume Salas also has had allegations of abuse laid against him). When Ziemann finally resigned, utterly disgraced, in 1999, Archbishop Levada praised him, without any mention of his sexual and financial misconduct. He had brought the diocese deeply into debt, to the tune of many millions (anywhere between $16 – 30 million, the amount is uncertain) because of his mismanagement. Quite apart from his personal sexually exploitative and abusive behaviour, Ziemann was also part of a cover-up of abuse allegations against priests in the Los Angeles archdioceses when he worked there.

When Ziemann resigned in 1999, William Levada ran the Santa Rosa diocese as an Apostolic Administrator for a year until a new bishop could be installed. In that time, his office refused to fully co-operate with the police and prosecutors, attempting to discourage any possible criminal charges against Ziemann. As a result he was able to be 'retired' to a pleasant retreat in Tombstone, Arizona. It is interesting to note that Ziemann's protectors: Cardinals O'Mahony of Los Angeles, William Levada of San Francisco and Bishop Manuel Moreno of Tuscon, Arizona, in whose diocese Ziemann was given refuge, all have appalling records with regard to the treatment of those who suffered at the hands of clerical sexual abuse of children and minors and the cover-up of the abuse (see www.bishop-accountability.org).

This gives some insight into the man who believed that he led the group that had the final say on Catholic doctrine, whose authority could not be questioned and who could punish without being called to account.

Seán felt utterly demeaned by the CDF's procedures and not only because of Cardinal Levada's questionable past. He was never directly and personally addressed by a representative of the dicastery as a priest and religious, over 82 years old, "who has given his whole life to the service of the Church, teaching, counselling and writing. ...When some Vatican communication comes *down to me*, it makes me feel like an impersonal piece of throwaway trash, not a human person." (*SF Dossier/ SF/JH/10-02*) [emphasis in original].

This put the Marist leadership in a difficult position. They wanted to save Seán from the ultimate sanction of being dismissed from priesthood, a sanction orchestrated by the man who praised a notorious abuser in former Bishop Patrick Ziemann, and protected him from civil authorities. In February 2010, while awaiting a response to the proposals they had set before Cardinal Levada and Msgr Charles Brown following the meeting of 18th January, the superior general wrote to Seán pleading with him not to publish anything. He emphasised again to Seán that most of his writings were known to the CDF, that the anonymous accuser(s) had carefully compiled and submitted a collection of key writings that they believed to be contrary to Catholic moral teaching.

Diocesan censor

In the meantime, following the publication of *What Happened to Sin?* and the reaction of the CDF when they heard of it, the book was submitted to the censor of the Dublin archdiocese. On the whole, the reaction to the book is quite benign. Where it can be praised it is, where there are difficulties these are highlighted. For anyone who has read *What Happened to Sin?* and had some misgivings about the wisdom of its publication, one cannot but say the censor's report was a fair assessment, not least when it says "...there are almost two books in the text, each struggling to come out: a repeat of the earlier one and a rather better and more pastorally inclined later one". The most significant comment on the book is that more recent Church teachings are not mentioned. This is true, but this was not disregard for these teachings, although Seán, like so many other moral theologians, would have had very serious reservations about *Veritatis Splendor* in particular. It was because *What Happened to Sin?* was an edited version of 1977 book *Has Sin Changed?* using more inclusive language with some extra comment here and there throughout the various chapters, and significant extensions of the two chapters on sex and on law, that left the later documents unexamined. That said, however, the report of the Dublin diocesan censor was hardly a damning indictment of the book. In fact, moral theologian, Fr Kevin T. Kelly says of the book: "It is a magnificent resource in the field of adult education, which is such a crying need today. I also love the way you constantly go back to Vatican II for your inspiration and to validate what you are saying. Congratulations, Seán, and many thanks for it. It is a crime that it is being withheld from ordinary lay-people who are hungry for such nourishing theology." (*SF Dossier/ KK/SF/10-12*).

Seán had great respect for his new superior general, Fr John Hannan. In a letter of 25th January 2010, he speaks of "all your kindness and for the special grace of your friendship". He also spoke to me very sympathetically of Fr Hannan's situation vis-à-vis the CDF in many of our conversations. It is obvious from the correspondence on the matter of the CDF's punishment of Seán that Fr John Hannan equally had great respect for Seán. He tried with difficulty and compassion to steer a path that would do the least damage to Seán, now heading towards his 83rd birthday. The question of collusion with injustice became an important issue for Seán. He said: "Traditional Catholic morality teaches that *cooperation in evil* is a serious sin. When the CDF continues to function as it did in the Inquisition, it is evil." (*SF Dossier/SF/JH/10-04*). Regardless of any understanding and sympathy regarding the difficulty of the circumstances, this remains an issue for the leadership of the Marists – to what extent did they 'cooperate in evil' and so bring such undeserved pain and suffering upon an elderly man. One can understand Seán's deep frustration with the process or, rather, the lack of process. He said in the same letter: "Talk of penalties and dismissal, with no reference to proper canonical procedures, brings back the infamous Inquisition, for which John Paul II 'apologised' after five hundred years."

Sword of Damocles

On 1st March, 2010, the sword of the CDF's ire that had been hanging over Seán since 1999 fell upon him. At the insistent demand of the CDF, the Marist leadership had to take the following action against Seán Fagan, *pro bono ecclesiae* [for the good of the Church]:

1. He was formally bound, under the vow of obedience, not to publish in the print media, not to speak on radio or television or otherwise propagate material against the faith and moral teachings of the Catholic Church as taught by the Magisterium.

2. He was asked under the same vow of obedience not to inform the media of the disciplinary procedures taken against him.

3. If he abided by these acts of obedience, he could continue to live his religious and priestly life unhindered. There would be no more action taken against him.

However, despite the already stringent nature of this action there were further caveats. If Seán infringed any of these stipulations, the Marist leadership was required by the CDF to prohibit him from exercising his priestly faculties:

- to celebrate the Eucharist in public and to preach
- to prepare people for, or to celebrate, the sacraments of baptism, penance, marriage and anointing

Furthermore, if the stipulations above were invoked, and Seán were to fail to abide by them, he would be dismissed from religious life. This would mean dismissal from his Marist family – essentially he would be rendered homeless as he would be dismissed from the congregation and no longer belong to the Marists.

Apart from the sanctions laid upon him and the threats of what would happen if he did not comply, there were two further 'requirements' of the CDF to be satisfied. The Marist Fathers in Ireland had to buy up all the remaining stock of *What Happened to Sin?* in the publisher's possession, and a notice had to be published on the Marist's Irish website that the book did not have the approval of, or represent the views of, the Society of Mary (The Marist Fathers).

This was all delivered to Seán in a private meeting at a venue away from his community residence by two of his confrères. Given what he already knew about Cardinal Levada's disgraceful record as a bishop in the U.S., it was not an easy burden, but in deference to his Marist leadership, and sympathy for their position, Seán accepted with his usual grace the burden laid upon him. Though he accepted with grace, the cost to him was very great. He struggled with the reality of the sanctions. His great spiritual gift – that of communication, always deployed in the service of the Church, was repudiated, without any recourse to justice.

In agreeing to the heavy burden laid upon him, Seán was at pains to assure his superior general that he was at peace with all that had gone on, because that was his intention. In truth, he was not at peace. Not at all. In an email of 9ᵗʰ March, 2010 he was very gracious to Fr John Hannan, as was his way. He genuinely tried to be as accepting of the situation as he could. However, he felt betrayed and was very angry. Not only because of the misuse of the vow of obedience, but also because of the difficult position in which Fr John Hannan found himself. Seán struggled to accommodate that anger and not let it destroy him. He used the safety valve of venting that anger to close friends. In an email exchange with Seán's legal advisor ten days after Seán's email to John Hannan accepting the punishment, I wrote the following:

> What is concerning me greatly now is to what extent am I colluding with an injustice? By saying nothing we are allowing the Vatican to break Seán's spirit. When Seán phoned me when the final word came though about his 'punishment' he was a broken man. I've never heard him so utterly depleted… it is the only word I can think of…. he sounded wrung out, exhausted and so, so very sad. It sounded as if his very will to live had been pierced.

CHAPTER NINE

Things to think about

Sometimes being a member of a religious order or congregation can be a protection for a priest from the attentions of the CDF, as in the case of Gustavo Gutiérrez, the 'father' of liberation theology. His struggle alongside the poorest people within South America and his efforts to empower them did not endear him to the Vatican. He was welcomed into the Dominican Order and thus more protected from the CDF than he had been previously as a diocesan priest. Other times, such as in Seán's case, it allows for moral blackmail – Seán's religious leader had to bear the brunt of the CDF's anger in the person of William Levada and that affected Seán both emotionally and intellectually. The case of Fr Peter Phan, a secular priest, is therefore quite interesting. For the details of this case, I am indebted to Fr Charles Curran who has generously shared with me the text of his lecture on Fr Phan and the CDF. This was given at a two-day symposium, *Theology Without Borders*, in Georgetown University, Washington, D.C., on 30th March, 2017. As yet this paper is unpublished.

Peter Phan's case

Fr Phan, Vietnamese by birth, arrived in the U.S. in 1975 as a refugee. He grew to maturity, and after a somewhat unconventional route to ordination, he became a priest and taught theology at highly-regarded universities. His early writings were on systematic theology. These did not cause any ripples and he gained a reputation as a serious and well-respected scholar. Over time he became interested in interfaith dialogue and, given his background, became especially interested in the study of Asian religions and Asian theology. In 2004 he published a book, *Being Religious Irreligiously: Asian perspectives on interfaith dialogue.*

As Fr Charlie points out in his essay, issues such as liberation theology and moral theology – especially on sexuality and marriage – had become 'hot button' issues in the post-Vatican II Church. In the early 2000s, interfaith dialogue became a new 'hot button' issue. According to the CDF, Phan's book did not conform to almost all the teaching of *Dominus Iesus*, Cardinal Ratzinger's 2000 document which pointed out that while non-Christians can be saved, non-Christian religions are gravely deficient in comparison with Christians who have the fullness of salvation. It should be noted here that *Dominus Iesus* was a shock to most theologians, and many other ecumenically-minded people within the Church, when promulgated and caused much upset. It was very damaging to interfaith relationships at the time and halted the welcome progress in interfaith dialogue.

Fr Phan's ordeal began in September 2005 when he received a set of *Observations* by the CDF on his book, accompanied by a letter dated 20th July. His bishop also received an instruction telling him what they wanted Fr Phan to do in his reply and the deadline given was six months (one assumes from July, the date of the covering letter). Phan's constructed 'reply' was to be in the form of an article to be submitted to the CDF for examination, which would then be published in a suitable theological journal. There was also a prohibition on the reprint of his book.

Given his many prior commitments and the delay in receiving the observations, Fr Phan asked his bishop to request an extension to the deadline to March 2006 from the CDF. By April 2006, Fr Phan had heard nothing regarding his case. He then wrote to Cardinal Levada, the Prefect of the CDF. He requested three things:

- that the prohibition on the reprint of his book be revoked – the prohibition presumed guilt before being able to defend his position
- clarification about the nature and scope of the article the CDF wanted him to write for publication
- fair and just remuneration for the work he would have to do to write the detailed article.

Fr Phan had to earn his own salary to live and he was also supporting his mother financially, therefore he asked the CDF to pay for half his annual salary since they had given him six months to write his response to their accusations. He would need to take that time off his paid employment to reply to them. He requested this to make the important point that now many theologians are lay people whose salary supports themselves and their families. Clerics such as curial cardinals are used to having all their material needs being taken care of, but other people have to work to earn enough for their needs. To Phan it was a matter of justice that there be fair recompense.

Selective silence

Phan heard no more from the CDF. They put the matter back into the hands of his bishop for appraisal by the U.S. Bishops' Committee on Doctrine. Why did the CDF withdraw from Phan's case? It is not difficult to conclude it was because they could not easily 'get' him – he was not an easy target. Also, he had the courage and confidence to put conditions to his response; to remind those in the CDF that in the real world bills have to be paid. In his informative essay, Fr Curran also discusses other cases and contrasts the behaviour and attitude of the CDF where they could and did put pressure on the leaders of religious orders and congregations. He further points out that two theologians, one clerical, one lay, wrote articles on homosexuality for the same theological journal in 2004. The priest's article did not question the official teaching on homosexuality, but he was investigated by the CDF and was obliged to issue a 'clarification'. The lay theologian raised issues about the official teaching on homosexuality but suffered no reprimand and no consequences.

This raises serious and fundamental issues about the behaviour and practices of the Congregation for the Doctrine of the Faith, about the fairness of its procedures, and about justice for those who are vulnerable to its predations. As an observer, one cannot help but get the impression it is a case of 'we'll get you, just because we can,' or that a lay Catholic's voice is of such little importance or such little value in its contribution to the Church, it does not even cause a ripple of concern.

Reform of the Curia was discussed during Vatican II, but nothing came of it apart from some consolidation of duties and responsibilities. The same thing has happened under the pontificate of Francis – there has been a temporary stay on the worst of its behaviour, but there has been nothing done to redress the injustices already caused and which continue to do harm. There has been no true reform, especially of the Congregation for the Doctrine of the Faith. The culture of the CDF means that its destructive and cruel exercise of power continues to perpetuate and has shown that it cannot be reformed. It is in a temporary abeyance at the moment in terms of its ferocity, but that is all. The Church managed to survive for 1,500 years before it decided that it needed an Inquisition. In the tradition of the Church, doctrinal disputes were dealt with through councils and synods. This allows a fruitful, if at times heated, collaboration between leaders and theologians for the good of the Church. Yet again, we see that the Church authorities are highly selective in what they choose to take from the tradition.

During his own doctrinal trial with the CDF on foot of anonymous accusers, the moralist Bernard Häring told the Prefect of the

Congregation in a letter that during the Second World War he was brought before a military court four times. On two of those occasions, it was a case of life or death for him. He said that he had no problem with that as the accusations against him were true: he was not submissive to the Nazi regime. But in this trial by the CDF, the accusations were untrue and he was being accused "in an extremely humiliating manner". Worse, they came from a senior department of leadership in a Church in which "I in a long life have served with all of my power and honesty and hope to serve still further with sacrifice". And then he made the most damning comment of all about his doctrinal trial and the behaviour of the CDF. He said: "I would rather stand once again before a court of war of Hitler." (*My Witness for the Church* pp.132-33).

Obedience

Given that Seán was bound to silence under his vow of obedience, we need to consider this. Obedience in religious life is, first and foremost, a vow of obedience to the gospel. It also has a function in the ordered living of the individual within community. The word for obedience in both Semitic and Indo-European languages is derived from the word 'to hear'. It always implies a willingness to listen to what the person in authority has to say and to act accordingly to undertake to do the will of that person. However, it is not simply meant to be interpreted in a militaristic way – order given and command obeyed – and the use of reason is not precluded from submitting to obedience. Human actions are virtuous to the extent that they are free. Submitting to obedience freely is entirely different to submitting to obedience under threat of sanction and punishment. It should be exercised, as far as possible on one's own responsibility – a person sees, understands, and accepts the reason for submitting one's will to obedience. It can be neatly encapsulated by "attention, reception and response" (Hinze, *Prophetic Obedience*, p.92).

Submission to obedience under duress is not true to the spirit of that counsel (poverty, chastity and obedience are called the evangelical counsels). "Power can be used to coerce compliance, but it is powerless to coerce obedience, since obedience depends on the consent of one who obeys." (Hauerwas & Pinches, *Christian Among the Virtues,* p.135). This truth about coercion is borne out by the contemporary renewal of religious life. Using the insights of modern psychology and sociology, obedience perceived as command/comply is understood to be very unhealthy. Such a model fosters surrender of personal decision-making and responsibility, as well as the moral immaturity that arises from always assuming that the leader of the community is responsible for one's choices and actions. (I am reminded of a friend in religious life who struggled in her patience with some of her contemporaries who were in the habit of saying: "Mother says..." as the infantile response to any and all discussions). Though there needs to be leadership in any organisation for it to function properly, that leadership does not have to be hierarchical or coercive. Such leadership is counter-productive, creating layers of superiority and inferiority, dominance and subservience, maternalism/paternalism and infantilism. None of which is healthy in adult groups and communities, regardless of what the settings of such communities are. Collaborative leadership is much more suited to a community of adults, where discernment plays a significant role.

One of the most important theological realisations of the renewal of religious life is that the Spirit speaks through all members of the community. To assume that somehow only the leader is the 'voice of God' is to diminish the role of the Spirit in the community and the search to discern the will of God for them as community and as "leaven in the world". The primary act of obedience in any recent literature on obedience in religious life is the obedience to the Word of God. This obedience reaches its fullest expression in the saying 'yes' to coming into being from God. Following from this fundamental 'yes', there is the 'yes' to a life conformed to the teaching of Jesus in the gospel. There is the 'yes' to the charism of the community and the living of that in the world. Through that living out of the charism, there is the 'yes' to the Spirit that moves and inspires other people from whom we have something to learn about God. And they can be some of the most unlikely people according to the standards of the world.

Obedience also applies to leaders and how they lead; it is not simply their being in charge and other people obeying. People in authority are called to serve an ideal that is greater than themselves. And that service is in communion with others, not above them. It is a communitarian effort to understand the movement of the Spirit. The obedience of leadership is also to keep the charism of the congregation alive and animated in the community. It is about remaining true to their founding ideals, the expression of which may change and evolve with time. Obedience in leadership requires that people in authority promote the dignity of the person and that each member is seen truly for themselves. It also means that the gifts to the service of the wider Church of the individual member be affirmed and encouraged. Obedience of leadership requires that a leader help those who struggle with difficulties, fostering courage and resilience. It requires depths of empathy that, in some instances, are not always well developed in religious life.

Obedience in religious life is a complex concept – it is not just the simple military-style command-and-obey or 'Mother says...'. In its theological development, it is now understood to be rooted in the Trinity. This is very important as the Trinitarian development is about relationship – God for us, who is God the Father/Mother; God alongside us who is both the Jesus who lived and died and the Christ who rose from the dead; God within us who is the Holy Spirit, the animator who wakes people up from the unthinking imitation of those around us and teaches us that tradition is the "living faith of the dead, and not the dead faith of the living". Obedience, then, grows from an inner conviction of relationship. A relationship, first and foremost, with God. Then, relationship within the community fostered by the community's charism. This progresses to the leader in relationship with the community and the community in relationship with the leader. Through the community and its charism, there is the relationship with the wider world. It is a web of relationships that have different emphases at different times, but ultimately, it is always about service. Service to the community and to the wider world animated by the relationship with God, who is the motivating imperative. The community at any given time is both freed and bound by this service, which is some ways is the paradox of obedience. As the theologian Bradford Hinze says:

> Prophetic obedience does not entail blind capitulation to authority, nor is it the mindless following of the populist mob. It requires heeding the signs of the times, honestly facing reality, and wrestling with it. Rather than succumbing to received opinions or accepted traditions, prophetic obedience tests and in certain cases interrogates these in the light of the living faith of the Church, recognised and received in the *sensus fidei*.
>
> (*The Tablet*, 03.06.2017) [Sensus fidei = the sense of faith of the people]

In this broader understanding of obedience and freedom, and of obedience and service, the CDF, obliging Seán, under his vow of obedience, to comply with its demands was clearly not in the spirit of the vow. It was a naked abuse of power. Seán did not write or communicate for his own purposes or his own vanity. He wrote because he felt compelled by his obedience to gospel, to the Word of God and obedience to the presence of the Spirit among the People of God. He listened carefully (remember, obedience comes from the Latin word to listen) to the people he served and, in the light of his own faith and his fidelity to the gospel, he strove to serve them as fully as he was able. As the Marists' own Constitution points out: "Obedience is sterile if it is cut off from love of God and neighbour. Charity brings Marists into communion with the risen Lord and with all believers, united in heart and mind, as they prepare for the coming of God's Kingdom." (MC, n.223).

In his later years, Seán saw his apostolate as pastor to the alienated – to the people wounded and hurt by the Church itself. In all of this he was obedient to his charism as a Marist, to his call as a priest, to his well-informed understanding of what it was to be a Catholic, to his formed and informed conscience, but ultimately to his God who was given flesh in the person of Jesus and gave humanity a template for living a good and decent life.

Canon Law

Canon law is the legal structure of the Church. It is meant to be more than just a legal framework for administrative purposes. It is also meant to further the message of the Church by encouraging the people to strive for a more perfect way of living and acting. The norms of canon law are not meant to be ends in themselves, but rather linked to authentic values, be they human and/or divine. Without such a link, no law can have authority. Whenever the law in itself, as law, takes precedence over faith, hope and love, it manifests rules for rules sake, which is "a permanent temptation for religious communities". As such it can mask itself as a semblance of faithfulness or obedience, but has a tendency to promote a type of rigid zealotry rather than show an understanding of the organic nature of community (Beal *et al.*, *Commentary on the Code of Canon Law* p.4).

The law is considered changeable and in constant need of reform inasmuch as it is a human instrument and displays all the weaknesses of that. It is considered constant insofar as it gives effect to the word of God. This was understood when at the close of Vatican II a commission was set up to revise the *Code of Canon Law*. A number of principles were agreed upon to guide the revision. Among these were: canon law should avoid excessive rigidity, those with pastoral care should have discretion in the application of the law; the principle of subsidiarity should be recognised, leaving plenty of 'wriggle room' for local and regional legislation; ecclesiastical penalties should be kept to a minimum and the code should be revised and restructured in conformity with the decrees of Vatican II.

Given that they are the result of human debate and deliberation, laws are fallible. Mistakes are made. Situations arise that could not have been anticipated when the laws were made. All laws are applied by people – they do not have an existence separate from those who have made them and those who apply and enforce them. Therefore, the attitudes of those who enforce the laws influence the effects of the law on others. A person with little or no imagination, with the type of personality that is highly rule-orientated, who rarely mixes socially and who keeps within his or her own tight group will apply the law one way. The person with a good imagination, widely-read, with a broad spectrum of friends and acquaintances, who sees rules more as a tool for good order than absolutes, will apply the law another way. If one is going to pass judgment on another, a rigorous self-knowledge would seem to be an important prerequisite. There was an understanding of this in the principles agreed for the reform of the *Code*. However, the bishops as a global group did not pay much attention to the revision of canon law. Opus Dei, on the other hand, placed considerable focus on it. Its university, the University of Navarra, became the foundation for a school of canon lawyers who took an active role from the very beginning in the Committee on the Renewal of Canon Law (Örsy, *Receiving the Council* p.86, n.21). The new *Code of Canon Law* was promulgated in 1983.

The observation of moral theologian Kevin T. Kelly is apt here. "What is the meaning of being human in the light of the best self-understanding of our age and what are the implications of this in real life?" (*50 Years of Receiving Vatican II*, p.114). To be truly *of* the community the law needs to grow out of the community's understanding of itself – what it is, why it exists, what values it holds, what its purpose is in the wider community, and what it hopes for itself and the wider community as life unfolds. In canon law there is a constant conflict between "the demand of stability and the imperative of development" (Örsy, *Receiving the Council* p.105). Communities evolve, the law needs to evolve with it or, as the canonist Ladislas Örsy, in a fine essay, puts it: "...the laws will break the community or the community will break the laws" (*The Art of Interpretation*). The Christian community is meant to be shaped by the gospels before anything else. This applies as much to canon law as any other aspect of church – perhaps more so, given the potential of the law, in certain hands, to become a dry, hardened legalism that omits to give weight to the complexities of the human situation. Canon law is a means to an end – an authentic living of a Christ-centred life. If the gospel message of Jesus ceases to be the standard by which the Church orders and reforms its life, that which is useful and worthy in the law will be discredited. It will be harmed by that which risks breaking the community through making an idol of the law.

It is disturbing to see how Seán could be punished by the abusive and incorrect application of canon law, yet where there are clear situations to implement mandatory dismissal under canon 695 §2, as in the case of the sexual abuse of religious sisters in at least 23 countries, there does not seem to be the same urgency to apply the law with equal rigour.

CHAPTER TEN

Silenced

On 3rd March, the instruction issued by the Marist superior general on 1st March, 2010, on foot of the ultimatum by the CDF, was delivered personally to Seán by two confrères, which included the local Irish superior. Given the inhumanity of the CDF's procedures, this at least showed some respect to Seán by giving him the sentence in person. From this day, he was forced to deny his charism as a theologian, without the justice of due process. He was under threat of being dismissed by the CDF not only from priesthood but from his congregation (essentially, a dismissal from his family and home at his then age of 83). He thus felt obliged to undertake a vow of silence imposed by this Vatican dicastery through his religious superior. To get some idea of this punishment, think of forbidding a musician to play or a poet to compose. In correspondence with Fr Hannan in May 2010 he said, "However unjust the Vatican 'procedures,' I hereby submit myself totally to them, not at all for the good of the Church which I love, but the protection of our dear Marist Society and my own personal integrity." (*SF Dossier/SF/JH/10-10*)

Not only that, he was also forced to accept that the penalty laid upon him be kept secret from the media and that he would be considered responsible if the media got hold of the story, even *without* Seán's knowledge or consent. One cannot emphasise enough the sense of fear this instilled in Seán – a man not easily intimated. Despite the Vatican's threat, Seán entrusted this story to a number of trustworthy people, including at least two journalists. He felt he owed them an explanation for his refusal to comment publicly on relevant matters. But he emphasised the importance of their discretion for his safety. It is heartening to note that those in the media who heard of the story had the integrity to hold back to protect an elderly man from eviction from his home – they didn't collude in this abuse for the sake of a story.

The Marist Congregation was obliged to buy up all remaining copies of his book *What Happened to Sin?* (800+ copies) to remove them from the public forum. Despite several requests, for quite a long time Seán was not told what happened to these books – were they destroyed? Were they in storage? This was a source of immense hurt to him – he felt he was being treated like a child by the local Marist leadership. He simply wanted reassurance that the books had not been destroyed and were in storage somewhere. Eventually, he was told they were in storage, but they would not tell him where. This was a wound that ran deep.

Seán Fagan did not lack courage, but it was his own cultural conditioning that prevented him from refusing to abide by the unjust burden laid upon him. He was, first and foremost, a loyal and devoted Marist. He was very disturbed that Fr John Hannan was treated so abominably by the CDF. He also understood the challenges of leadership and felt bad that he was the cause of such difficulty for Fr Hannan just as he took over leadership of the worldwide Marist family. He also worried about the shame his own family would likely experience if he were dismissed, not only from priesthood but from his Marist family. There would be a deep shadow cast over his good name and the Fagan name generally. That was a very real worry for him. When the theologian, Kevin T. Kelly, whom Seán had known for decades, wanted to find a way to blow the whistle without actually mentioning Seán, so disgusted was he by his treatment, Seán demurred:

I share your feelings totally, but my family and friends ...
would be greatly perturbed by my being 'de-frocked' as the
Irish expression has it, deprived of my priesthood. I want to
protect them from that, hence my concern that my name or
my case should not come into the public domain. Were it not
for this deep concern I would have hesitation in accepting the
Vatican punishment and living with it for the rest of my life to
publicise their bullying inhumanity.

(*SF Dossier/SF/KK/*10-13)

But, there was also the fact that Seán was a priest to his marrow.
He truly did not know how to be anything else. By 2010, aged 83, he
had given the Church and 'God's Holy People' almost 60 years of
faithful ministry. This fidelity was not reciprocated in the application of due process by the Church's administration to Seán's case.
If a condemned man cannot hope for justice within the Church he
served so faithfully and so well, where does he turn? For Seán Fagan,
the answer was an emphatic 'nowhere' except to the support of
friends, with which he was abundantly blessed. They attenuated but
could not remove the shattering effect of the CDF's sanction on him.

Be vigilant

Towards the end of March 2010, a person close to the case
advised Seán to "be vigilant". He believed that the CDF could
not have all the information it possessed without it coming from
those "with easy access to your thinking and writing". Given the
fact that, between 2008 and 2010, Seán was mainly talking to
closed groups of various reform-minded Catholics, this warning
raised the ugly prospect that someone who pretended to share
his hope for reform was a wolf in sheep's clothing. This person
was secretly reporting to the CDF either directly or, Seán himself
suspected, as a spylet who operated in the darkness of deception

liaising with the spy who had direct contact with the CDF, to cause as much damage as possible.

The vigilance on the behalf of the Marists with regard to Seán's writings extended to his wish to pass on copies of the book to family members. It was not allowed. As Seán said when trying to get his hands on a few copies of *What Happened to Sin?* as gifts for his nieces and nephews:

> I have only one copy of the dangerous book, so I must not lose it or there will be no possibility of replacing it. If I made presents of it to nephews or nieces I don't know how Levada would hear about it, since the anonymous sick Vatican spy here would not know about it [being allowed to give the book to family only]. It is so sickening to have to beware at every moment of his presence and twisted mind. His species is encouraged by the Vatican's own culture of secrecy, spying, denouncing and punishing, with no reference whatever to the gospel, to the facts or to truth. ... They seem to think even a single copy could be explosive!
>
> ... The diabolical behaviour of the Vatican makes no sense except in the unnatural environment of Rome. Having enjoyed 27 years in Rome, I have no temptation to ever see it again. As for the ecclesiastical world, it would turn my stomach to see all the fancy dress and hear the silly titles that have become so essential to the Roman Church. When we have no scruple about totally disobeying the clear words of Jesus about titles, it should come as no surprise that our official leaders have no scruple about ignoring the gospel itself.
>
> (*SF Dossier/SF/EP-jh/10-08*)

In an email to Fr John Hannan, in June 2010, following contact from a fellow Marist in New Zealand affirming Seán, he said:

I try not to think of them [the CDF and Vatican authorities], they are so far removed from Jesus and the gospel, not to mention from civil society in today's world. It's no surprise that they are emptying the Church when they seem more interested in silk robes, the Latin Mass, wavering Anglican bishops and East-facing altars than in examining why our Church has not been a safe environment for its most vulnerable members, the children who have been abused in their thousands. How is it God's will that the Church is not open and transparent, but is reduced to a hard unfeeling body where power and decision-making are the preserve of elderly, celibate males with little experience of human relationships or even of Jesus and the gospel.

(*SF Dossier* /SF/JH/10-11)

The gospel was always Seán's yardstick for behaviour. He measured himself by it and he measured other people in positions of leadership by it, particularly the clergy. For Seán there was always a higher standard demanded of priests and bishops. They were supposed to lead by example; fidelity to the gospel values of humility, service and lifting burdens laid on the shoulders of others should always be to the fore. One could not profess the gospel and be involved in, or conceal matters around child abuse by clergy – Seán was trenchant in his opinion about that.

The biggest problem for the CDF was that Seán wrote in a very accessible way so that the non-specialist reader could understand his work (ordinary priests and catechists were mentioned). They admitted as much during one of the sessions with the Marist leadership – Seán was dangerous for the very reason that he could write plainly, succinctly and in a very accessible manner. He could reach a wide audience in the Church. As one lifetime friend of Seán (a Dominican priest) said after he told him the news of the silencing:

A little comfort. I can and do say, Seán, and you are fully aware of it – your Jesus-inspired, thoroughly Christian theology has helped and comforted, and continues to comfort, because your books have sold so well, to so very many people. You may be silenced; they can't silence the word that is out there.

(*SF Dossier*/WH/SF/10-7.5)

Stress problems

There were times, during all this, when Seán had suicidal ideation. Those close to him understood that he would not have acted on it, but he certainly spoke of it. It was a measure of his distress more than his intention. In the time between 2008 and 2010 he expressed many times the wish that he might go to bed one night and simply not wake up in the morning. At times he even prayed this would be so. In a letter to Fr Jim Good in October 2008 he recounted a recent event where he collapsed in his room and was there for two hours before being discovered. He thought he was having a heart attack and was convinced it was his last day and "was quite happy, just praying quietly 'Father, into your hands I commend my spirit'" until he was found and brought by ambulance to hospital. He was released six hours later without there being any definite diagnosis, but vertigo was mentioned as a mostly likely cause. He said to Fr Jim, "I am happy with the reprieve, but a bit sad having to wait".

He expressed this readiness to go to his death more vocally and regularly to me in the years following his punishment from the CDF in 2010 to shortly before he went to full-time nursing home residence. It was a struggle for him to say "it is good to be here" – something he could say for most of life, in good times and bad. And for a number of years he could not say that. However, the kindness and care he received in Cherryfield Nursing Home finally gave him the chance to think in those terms once again. Fr Gabriel Daly OSA, a long-time friend, spoke of Seán at a gathering of friends on the occasion of the first anniversary of his death. He spoke of Seán's great effort to forgive his accusers and tormentors and in the months before his death he managed to achieve this great charity and once again could say "it is good to be here".

Seán's situation was not helped by having had a run of accidents and illnesses. During the time when the Vatican attention was at its highest in the 2000s, Seán had several falls. Then, when threats eased off for a period, there were no more falls. For those close to him, we could see a direct correlation between the falls and the Vatican pressure. In 2003 he had shingles. He also had two severe bouts of cellulitis for which he was hospitalised. He suffered from vertigo and needed medication for high blood pressure amongst other things, and also had diabetes. He had prostate and thyroid problems. He had a bout of Bell's Palsy in 2005. He had surgery for cataracts – one which worked perfectly, but one which left him worse off in the sight of one eye, which made reading tiring. Three days before Christmas in 2009, just two months before the punishment was meted out, he was knocked down not far from his home in Leeson St. Luckily, the car was turning into a laneway and not travelling fast. Yet, it was no small thing at 82 years of age to be knocked down. He had no broken bones, but suffered very painful ligament and tendon damage to his right shoulder, arm and both knees. He suffered months of pain as a result. Fr John Hannan, in his attempts to plead Seán's case with the CDF, pointed out all his health difficulties together with his age, and the potential effect of their punishment but to no avail. There was no allowance for age or infirmity.

Given all this focus on the danger Seán posed to the Irish Church, it is to the great credit of those on the committee of the Association of Catholic Priests that they arranged a special presentation to Seán on 4th October 2011 at their AGM. This acknowledgement by his peers meant much to Seán and he treasured dearly the specially engraved crystal chalice that was presented to him, with the inscription:

Sean Fagan

Moral Theologian

Courageously serving the truth

It was a timely and humane act.

Reader in moral theology

Coinciding with this silencing of Seán Fagan by the CDF, was the preparation of volume two of a very important three-volume work edited by moral theologians Vincent McNamara and Enda McDonagh: *An Irish Reader in Moral Theology: the legacy of the last fifty years*, published by The Columba Press in 2011. The *Reader* consisted of an already-published first volume on the foundations of moral theology. This second volume was on sex, marriage and the family, which covered Seán's area of expertise. The purpose of the *Reader* was to gather in one easily-accessible place, the work of theologians that had made a significant contribution to discussion on morality over the past 50 years. During that time, Seán had very many articles published; articles which did not cause a ripple of controversy. Given Seán's standing within the Irish theological community, and his significant contribution to theology, it would be unthinkable that he would not be included in such a prestigious and important publication. After all, this work is intended be a resource for moral theology students for years to come, in following the trajectory of the development of moral theology within the Church. Given that the editors were choosing only published material, it would seem that there should be no reason to exclude Seán. However, given the strictures of the CDF ban on his work, and how they had reacted to his chapter in the *Response to the Ryan Report*, which was simply a factual recounting of the historical background, Seán's legal advocate advised against use of any of his previously published work. That the material was already in the public domain and had not attracted the Vatican's ire in the past was no comfort. Seán was a sitting target. The editors knew and understood this, and yet it would be an injustice to exclude him without comment. To future readers it would seem as if he was not worthy of consideration, which would make his then 53 years of ordained priestly service to the Church as nothing. Yet, they could not explain *why* he was not included, because it was made clear to Seán that if the fact of his punishment became known, *even without* his co-operation, he would be dismissed from the Marists. The editors, too, had their own problems. The *Reader* was to be published by Veritas Publications, but "last minute ecclesiastical interference with the publication of Volume I" meant they had to find a last-minute publisher. The indomitable Seán O'Boyle stepped in and saved the day and this great collection was published by The Columba Press. In the introduction where they mention this "ecclesiastical interference" they say:

> We had hoped to include some articles by moral theologian, Seán Fagan SM but 'due to circumstances outside our control' this was not possible. Given our experience of last minute ecclesiastical interference with the publication of Volume I, *Foundations*, and our consequent need to find an alternative publisher, it is hard to believe that this volume will escape some controversy. If the criticism is presented fairly and, above all, openly, allowing for genuine debate, then truth, moral theology and the Church can only benefit.

It is to be hoped that the positioning of Seán's name within that context was deliberate, so that anyone with eyes to see could read between the lines.

One hopes that in any future re-prints or new editions of the *Reader*, some of Seán Fagan's legacy will be included.

Helplessness

There was a feeling of anger and helplessness among those of us who knew what had happened to Seán. Not many knew of the details of his case, but theologians who know the workings of the CDF and who knew of colleagues, confrères and friends suffering a similar fate, felt great empathy for Seán. But that was accompanied by a sense of helplessness, again from knowledge of the CDF's methods. Any efforts to publicly support Seán were likely to rebound on him directly, incurring yet further suffering.

In a response to previous correspondence from Seán, the moral theologian Kevin T. Kelly says:

> I was deeply distressed and appalled to read about the disgraceful way you have been treated by the CDF. It is a horrendous example of the kind of 'God abuse' I was talking about [in a paper at an international conference]. ... It is a scandal that the CDF treats theologians 'as if people do not matter' and cannot see that the whole thrust of people like yourself is to develop a 'moral theology as if people matter'.
>
> ...To my mind the most scandalous injustice lies in your being silenced under your vow of obedience and especially in your being forbidden to inform the media of the disciplinary procedures taken against you – with the dire threat of your being dismissed from religious life and being banned from exercising your priesthood. To act in this way in the name of God is a blatant example of 'God abuse'.

> (*SF Dossier/KK/SF/*10-12)

Seán replied:

> I understand and appreciate your feelings of indignation about
> my case, and I share your concern about standing idly by and
> doing nothing. I have long pondered this and have come to the
> conclusion that there is nothing we can do to bring about any
> change. For centuries they have closed ranks and ignored any
> criticism, knowing that they have time on their hands. *Roma
> aeterna, transit mundus.* ... They have punished most major
> theologians for decades... I feel exactly as your good self about
> doing something, indeed feel guilty about *not* doing anything,
> but we are up against a Goliath, with time on his hands, a giant
> who will still be there long after we have gone. All we can do
> is to highlight the unchristian, indeed diabolical, situation and
> practice of the Vatican so that eventually the disgust of God's
> holy people may force them towards a little humility.

(SF Dossier/SF/KK/10-13)

Exiled

At the end of July 2011 Seán was moved to the Marist headquarters
in Ireland, Mount St Mary's, Milltown, Dublin. This was a planned
move as the house in Leeson St. was needed to expand their secondary school, the C.U.S. This was a very stressful move for Seán. It
signalled his separation from a normal life.

Having been silenced, Seán insisted that his books, which had
been bequeathed in his Will to The Priory Institute, Dublin, be
handed over before his physical death. His theological death made
this an imperative. If Seán could not write, he saw no point in keeping
his books after his move, despite my own attempts to persuade him
to the contrary. Ever practical, Seán thought it was a waste of time
packing and moving all the books to Milltown – what use were they to
him? His life had been taken away so the books had no function. On

19th July, 2011 he handed over this generous gift to the Priory Institute. It formed the solid basis for a library which has grown extensively since. Having been responsible for, and participated in, the removal of all Seán's books with Martin Cogan of the Priory Institute, it was like dividing the lots and numbering the bones.

Seán, who was always obedient to the call of his Marist life, was preparing himself for the final stage. He saw the move to Milltown as an exile – his life's work was now over. Mount St Mary's was the next to last stop, in his mind. He felt very isolated there and found getting in and out of the city awkward as the bus service was infrequent. While living in Leeson St he could pop into the city any time he wanted, which was good for his mental and emotional well-being. He was encouraged to take a taxi if he needed to get into town, but this is to miss the point – his freedom to move and come and go spontaneously was restricted because of the transport problems. Also, he regarded use of a taxi as a selfish extravagance if he just wanted to go to the city for a bit of shopping or to visit a bookshop. As he used to say: "If you need it, the society will provide it. If you don't need it, you shouldn't have it." Given his own standards, he did not see use of a taxi as a 'need'. And if he didn't need it, he shouldn't have it. So he did not. He was quite lonely, despite friends calling to see him from time to time.

After approximately two years in the house in Mount St Mary's, Milltown, in early 2014 Seán had to go into nursing home care, first in a temporary capacity but then permanently, in the Jesuit-run Cherryfield Nursing Home in Milltown. He was extremely well-cared for here, and was loved and respected by the staff. Those friends who regularly visited had nothing but praise for those who looked after Seán in Cherryfield, and for the beautiful environment created there.

And what of the vocation of the theologian?

In 1990 the CDF promulgated an *Instruction* on the ecclesial vocation of the theologian – *Donum Veritatis* (the gift of truth). It is 12 pages long, containing 43 articles, but can be summed up in one sentence: that the theologian's job is to present what the magisterium teaches. There is lip service paid to freedom of academic research, but when all is said and done, 'creeping infallibility' is the hallmark of this document. Over the pontificates of John Paul II and Benedict XVI, all teaching is linked in some way to revelation, and as the magisterium claims full competence with regard to revelation, therefore, by association it claims competence over all theology. This all-encompassing claim on competencies is the source of 'creeping infallibility'. Though *Donum Veritatis* acknowledges in a.31:

> It can also happen that at the conclusion of a serious study, undertaken with the desire to heed the magisterium's teaching without hesitation, the theologian's difficulty remains because the arguments to the contrary seem more persuasive to him. Faced with a proposition to which he feels he cannot give his intellectual assent, the theologian nevertheless has the duty to remain open to a deeper examination of the question.

It then states:

> For a loyal spirit, animated by love for the Church, such a situation can certainly prove a difficult trial. It can be a call to suffer for the truth, in silence and in prayer, but with the certainty, that if the truth is really at stake, it will ultimately prevail.

How can truth ultimately prevail, when efforts to arrive at truth that do not align with a particular attitude in the Vatican are stifled?

When the people who attempt to discern the truth are silenced, on threat of being rendered homeless without a means of support? Here we can see, unmasked, the embedded dysfunction in the Church – it is a tacit acknowledgment that they can get it wrong – but if so, they have no intention of admitting it. It will be up to the Church of the future to deal with present errors. In the meantime, it consciously and willingly forces sincere, faithful men and women to suffer in silence so that they, the authorities, do not have to admit they are wrong. There is not the slightest hint anywhere in the document that the magisterium of the Church has *anything* to learn from the skill, competence and faithfulness of theologians. There is no understanding that a moral tradition can be corrupted by individual and group bias. No understanding that a powerful individual or group of individuals will "given time and opportunity favour traditions that support and enhance their power over others" (Barden & Murphy, *Law & Justice in Community* p.63). Not only is there no insight or understanding of the human bias, but *Donum Veritatis* claims in article 37 that:

> The fact that these procedures [the investigations] can be improved does not mean that they are contrary to justice and right. To speak in this instance of a violation of human rights is out of place for it indicates a failure to recognise the proper hierarchy of these rights as well as the nature of the ecclesial community and her common good.

Fundamental human rights with regard to due process simply do not apply. How, then, can a Church which maintains that fundamental human rights to not apply to its own processes expect anyone to listen to it and take it seriously?

Justice in the world

It is timely here to quote a little from the synodal document *Justice in the World* from the 1971 Synod of Bishops. This was the first properly collegial meeting of world bishops following the Second Vatican Council. It is no accident that its first collaborative document was about justice. Then, as now, there were many injustices in the world to be challenged. The bishops of the synod saw that they had a role to challenge the prevailing systems of injustices. It took seriously the "Church's vocation to be present in the heart of the world by proclaiming the Good News to the poor, freedom to the oppressed, and joy to the afflicted". They saw that any attempts to transform the world had to be actions on justice which they saw "as a constitutive dimension of preaching the gospel" and the Church's mission for the liberation of people from every oppressive situation.

This is a small document, a pamphlet of only 21 pages, but it is very comprehensive in its vision of justice for and in the world. In section II, it states that the gospel mandate to preach justice is why the Church needs to witness justice in its own institutions. More explicitly, it says in section III:

> While the Church is bound to give witness to justice, she recognises that anyone who ventures to speak to people about justice must first be just in their eyes. Hence we must undertake an examination of the modes of acting and of the possessions and life style found with the Church itself...

> The Church recognises everyone's right to suitable freedom of expression and thought. This includes the right of everyone to be heard in a spirit of dialogue which preserves a legitimate diversity within the Church. ...

The form of judicial procedure should give the accused the right
to know his accusers and also the right to a proper defence.

Furthermore, at the end of section III we are told:

The examination of conscience which we have made together
regarding the Church's involvement in action for justice will
remain ineffective if it is not given flesh in the life of our local
Churches at all their levels.

And, in the thrust and tone of the whole document, one should
also say: and the Church administration at all its levels. The declara-
tions of the Church in the past tend now to be reassessed by the per-
ceptive reader in the light of the appalling scandal of clerical sexual
abuse of children and the persistent cover-up by bishops. That said,
the words of this document on justice are still relevant, and never
more so than in relation to clerical child sexual abuse. However, they
are relevant to any case where justice is trampled upon. They are
relevant in Seán Fagan's case.

The freedom of this Synod in 1971 is reflected in the quality of
the document. It is clear, concise and its message easily accessed.
It sets out the fundamental points and trusts the local churches to
then use it as a working document for their own pastoral letters on
justice. Compared to the verbosity of many later papal and synodal
documents which constantly attempt to anticipate and close off any
contrary arguments, the 1971 Synodal document is an example of
best practice in collegiality.

Kevin T. Kelly, in his book *50 Years of Receiving Vatican II*, says that
teaching, in itself, is a moral activity. That teaching is immoral if:

it fails to respect the dignity of those being taught, abuses
their freedom, imposes the teaching on them, regardless of

whether they are able to accept or appreciate its truth and even punishes them for non-acceptance of what is being taught. ... It stifles healthy critical questioning, inhibits and cripples their creativity, quenches their spirit, and is profoundly anti-gospel. Such immoral use of teaching authority in the Church is unworthy of the Church. ... Part of the renewal of the Church would seem to be moving from an exercise of teaching authority based on domination and control to one based on loving service and empowering leadership (p.194).

For further insight into the importance of dialogue and discussion for a healthy Church, Richard McCormick's excellent book *The Critical Calling: reflections on moral dilemmas since Vatican II* is very helpful, especially chapter 4: 'The Chill factor in contemporary moral theology'. This book dates from 1989 and is as relevant today as it was at the time of publication. Also, Jim Corkery SJ, who has made a study of Joseph Ratzinger's theological ideas, has a very useful article 'Theological dissent' in *Doctrine & Life*, Jan 2007.

Criticism – part of the tradition

The tragedy is that, within the tradition of the Church, criticism, and sometimes very trenchant criticism especially in the medieval Church, had its place. This was so even in the nascent church. Paul had a confrontation with Peter in Galatia about the circumcision of Gentiles. We have Paul, a worker in and for the Church, challenging Peter the named leader by Jesus of the Church. This divine sanction was no barrier to Paul in his argument with Peter. It was not a reason to be nervous or diffident about the challenge. Likewise, the medieval critics were loyal churchmen but had no fear of scandalising the faithful with their critique. They understood something that more recent churchmen seem not to understand: the people have eyes to see and ears to hear. They have already been scandalised by what they have seen and heard. Speaking the truth to power does not scandalise the ecclesial community, it is simply embodying the gospel.

Pope Hadrian VI was elected in 1522 in a time of great turmoil for the Church and European politics. They were the very early years of the Protestant Reformation. Going by the example of recent Church history, one might expect defensiveness and affirmation of the *status quo* by the newly elected Pope, given the political and ecclesiastical upheaval. In a message given to a legate to the Diet of Nuremburg, where he demanded severe action with regard to Martin Luther, to suppress his revolt against the Church, Hadrian VI had no difficulty acknowledging the Church's blame in events leading to Martin Luther's actions (though he was viciously critical of Luther). He said:

> We know well that for many years things deserving of the abhorrence have gathered around the Holy See; sacred things have been misused, ordinances transgressed, so that in everything there has been a change for the worse. Thus it is not surprising that the malady has crept down from the head to the members, from the popes to the hierarchy.
>
> We all, prelates and clergy, have gone astray from the right way, and for a long time there is none that has done good. ...Therefore, in our name, give promises that we shall use all diligence to reform before all things the Roman Curia, whence, perhaps, all these evils have had their origins; thus healing will begin at the source of the sickness... We desire to wield our power not as seeking domination or means for enriching our kindred, but in order to restore to Christ's bride, the Church, her former beauty, to give help to the oppressed, to uplift men of virtue and learning, above all, to do all that beseems a good shepherd and a successor of the blessed Peter.

(Pastor, *The History of the Popes,* Vol 9, pp.134-35)

Hadrian did not last long enough in office to achieve any worth-while reform – he died in 1523. Much of the medieval Church critique was about the greed of the bishops and clergy for wealth and status. The criticism was overt and strong. Those writing were loyal church-men (and the very rare churchwomen) and not perceived enemies of the Church. Hadrian VI's comment above is just one simple example of many that exist spanning several hundred years. They included people such as Bernard of Clairvaux, Catherine of Siena, Brigid of Sweden and senior clerics such as William of Auvergne, Gerhoh of Reichersberg and Hilary of Poitiers, to mention a few. It is surpris-ing to see how often, how many and how trenchant, were the calls to reform. All of these were ignored by the ruling elite of the Church, thus leading to the great schism of the Protestant Reformation in the 16th Century.

This useful freedom of speech was circumscribed in the post-Ref-ormation until it became almost impossible, by the 19th Century, to make any helpful criticism of the Catholic Church. This state of affairs pertained right up to the Second Vatican Council (1962-65). Despite the reforms of Vatican II, it was a state that increasingly became the norm again under John Paul II and Benedict XVI and still remains, though with less emphasis on punishment, under Francis.

This enclosed way of thinking was commented upon by Karl Rahner in 1964:

> There are, in fact, earnest Catholics who are anxious to have a right mind about the Church and who hold the view... that the hierarchy is the only vehicle of the Spirit or the only portal through which the Spirit visits the Church. ... We must distin-guish between what we may perhaps... call an absolute claim made by the Church, valid within certain limits and strictly circumscribed, and a totalitarian conception of the Church...

... Ultimately, only one thing can give unity in the Church on a human level: the love which allows one another to be different, even when it does not understand him.... The principle that charity brings with it implies that each in the Church may follow his spirit as long as it is not established that he is yielding to what is contrary to the Spirit; that, therefore, orthodoxy, freedom and goodwill are to be taken for granted and not the opposite. Those are not only self-evident human maxims of a sensible common life built on respect and tolerance for others, but also principles which are very deeply rooted in the very nature of the Church and must be so. For they follow from the fact that the Church is not a totalitarian system. Patience, tolerance, leaving another to do as he pleases so long as the error of his action is not established – and not the other way round, prohibition of all individual initiative until its legitimacy has been formally proved, with the onus of proof laid on the subordinate – are, therefore, specifically ecclesiastical virtues springing from the very nature of the Church.

(Rahner, *The Dynamic Element in the Church*, pp.48-81 – esp. 70s)

Reading the document on the ecclesial vocation of the theologian, it is very clear that the kind of healthy exploration advocated by Karl Rahner 26 years before *Donum Veritatis* is not at all encouraged. The Church as a body has suffered as a result, because a Church that cannot encourage freedom of exploration of theology and, if anything, seems afraid of such exploration, has become a totalitarian Church that brooks no legitimate and loyal dissent. It does not require advanced degrees in theology or philosophy to understand that if there is a likelihood of error, any Church teaching can only benefit from public discussion within the ecclesial community, and especially among theologians. What is there to fear in seeking to find the truth of a matter by honest searching and dialogue? If there is no discussion there can be no growth, and if there is no growth, there is not stasis – there is decay.

CHAPTER ELEVEN

Seán Fagan - Marist priest

At the 1990 Synod on priestly formation, Bishop Derek Warlock of Liverpool, who spoke in the name of the bishops of England and Wales said: "Evangelisation begins with the conversion of the evangeliser to the good news of the gospel." He further emphasised the importance of a deep spirituality for priests and the motivation within the priest to develop such a spirituality for himself. Ecumenism, according to the bishops' document, was an essential element in the evangelising commitment. It also encouraged an openness to society and culture and a movement away from an often unacknowledged fear of the modern world. Priests had to be helped to "know and love human society," which required a fundamental understanding of the cultural needs of the local community, which will vary significantly between continents, between nations, even within parts of a nation.

What a priest is meant to be

The priest or religious is a person who is meant to be other-centred, and to serve in such a way. Inculturation is a necessary part of the process of serving the People of God. Seán Fagan had an innate sense of People of God ecclesiology and the importance of inculturation. If he was going to embody the good news of the gospel, he had to meet people where they were, in the reality of their day-to-day lives. And his guide for this encounter throughout his whole life was Jesus, as portrayed in the gospel and the Christ of the resurrection. Joan Chittister calls this "following a beckoning God". To be faithful to this path does not mean preserving the past unchanged. It is not "a stability of place; it is a stability of heart".

When one reads the *Decree on the Ministry and Life of Priests* (*Presbyterorum Ordinis*) from Vatican II, one is constantly reminded as to how Seán Fagan conformed to the best that might be hoped for in a priest. He certainly cultivated "those virtues which are rightly held in high esteem in human relations. Such qualities are goodness of heart, sincerity, strength and constancy of mind, careful attention to justice, courtesy..." and quoting from St Paul's letter to Philemon, other qualities such as whatever is true, honourable, just, pure, lovely, gracious... (*PO*, n.3). Again, "..the priest's preaching, often very difficult in present-day conditions, if it is to become more effective in moving the minds of his hearers, must expound the Word of God, not merely in a general and abstract way but by an application of the eternal truth of the gospel to the concrete circumstances of life." (*PO*, n.4). Furthermore, "He is able to discover and carry out that will [of God] in the course of his daily routine by humbly placing himself at the service of all those who are entrusted to his care by God in the office that has been committed to him and the variety of events that make up his life." (*PO*, n.15). Again and again, in reading the Vatican II *Decree*, allowing for a certain amount of dating of the document, one sees how fully Seán Fagan personified all that was best and desirable in a priest/pastor.

It's good to be here

This is also seen in his own three favourites of the prodigious number of articles he had written: *It's good to be here, Sacraments in the spiritual life* and *Nobody grows alone;* published 1971, 1974 and 1986, respectively. Seán was a very practical man. That is not to say he did not have imagination, he valued poetry and art, but he was very focused on the real struggle and problems many people have just trying to live their lives. It was this awareness that comes through in these three articles. He saw the revelation of God in the everyday. "It is not a question of mystical experience or private revelation, but simply the Christian duty to read the signs of the times as indications of God's will." It is our duty as Christians to see the world through the "eyes of faith, in the light of the gospel and recognise God's will, God's call... in the requirements of the present moment". He says that if God were to indicate his will in a formal solemn way, we would have no problem. However, it is not quite so easy to discern that same will "in the need of a troublesome neighbour, the boring task to be done, the impatient waiting on something beyond our control".

If we can see the world in this way, then each moment is not merely a sign but a channel of God's grace, "an opportunity for encounter with Christ". For Seán "every moment is the right moment for God". This includes self-acceptance, "with our ailments, our failures, our discouragements, our sufferings, our weakness, our shame, our loneliness". He acknowledges that it is easy to say "Lord, it's good to be here" when things are going well, in times of consolation, in times of pleasure and satisfaction. But the "real test is to be able to repeat the same words with naked will when our natural wish is to be elsewhere". Seán accepted that it is natural to want to be elsewhere when things are tough, but this is when the spirit of faith comes into play. For him, the person's act of will, the personal commitment to faith always plays a crucial role. If we appreciate what the sacrament of the present moment means in times of joy and happiness, then "this cultivated habit will prepare us for the big moments, the important decisions calling for a special act of faith". For the times when it is almost impossible to say 'Lord, it is good to be here' but yet we can still say it and mean it. Seán, following Thomas Aquinas, firmly believed that the practice of the virtues, such as temperance, patience, prudence, and justice, eventually made a person virtuous.

Sacraments in the spiritual life

Seán was very uncomfortable with what could be described as 'magical thinking' when it came to the sacraments in the spiritual life. The older way of thinking of sacraments was almost as sort of a holy power to re-charge the spiritual batteries, enabling a person to live in the world "without being contaminated by it". For Seán, all creation was holy. There were no separate sacred and profane worlds. The divine life and grace is everywhere, whenever and wherever humankind does not close itself to God by "culpably rejecting grace". He situated sacraments in the spiritual life in this context. They are not magic conduits of grace to buttress our faith against the world. They are high points or peak moments related to life as a whole, they are "not irruptions from a different world". They enlarge our vision and so bring us into deeper meaning of life. They help us focus on what we might ignore in the ordinary, everyday busyness of life. This is not to say that the world is of God and there is nothing more to be said. Rather, as Christians we accept that here "we have no lasting city", we are a pilgrim people stumbling along our way but our ultimate destination is with God. However, it is through the community of the faithful we have contact with Christ, and in a special way in the sacraments. They are ecclesial, communal events not private encounters with Christ, something that is not always fully appreciated. They are signs of faith in three ways. "Firstly, insofar as they *express the faith of the Church*" in particular gestures and words the community believes it offers a real mediation of our encounter with God. "Secondly, insofar as they demand from the recipient a *response of faith*" which is necessary for the encounter with God. "Finally, insofar as the sacramental rite, with the words, are accompanied by a *gift of faith*" a gift of the Holy Spirit, without which the Church could not make its gesture of faith, nor could we be capable of our response of faith.

In his understanding of sacraments in the spiritual life, Seán also acknowledges that the secondary symbols of the sacraments, the various rites, gestures, words, etc., have been "used by the Church in the course of history". In other words, they are culturally conditioned. They grew out of specific cultural milieux. The primary symbols of sacrament (birth, growth to maturity, table fellowship, marriage, illness, death, etc.) remain stable, but the secondary symbols may lose their significance when the cultural and historic context changes. Seán understood, when he wrote about this in 1974, that there were significant cultural changes afoot and the Church needed to be alert to these. He asked: "Can we be satisfied with a static liturgy for a dynamic culture?" He also understood that to bring home more forcefully the primary symbols of the sacraments, some of the secondary symbols may need to change.

He was also uneasy with what he called "the mathematical approach" to sacraments, especially with regard to an "exaggerated insistence" on frequency. "Quality must always come before quantity, and quality implies a genuine response in faith." God's love is without bounds and so much greater than anything of which a human being might conceive. This deeper understanding of the encounter with God is the purpose of sacrament, not as "slot machines to produce grace".

Nobody grows alone

That nobody grows alone, that we are what our relationships allow us to be, was fundamental to Seán's worldview. We need each other, not only to produce the practical goods and services needed for us to live and function well, but we need each other to grow as human beings. The idea of the self-made person being the ideal of human achievement was to him a contradiction in terms. Human beings need each other. This is not just a psychological insight, but a fundamental Christian insight – the commandment to love one another is considered the most important of all. It is in and through our actions and interactions with others that we realise the Christian life. Seán had the capacity for relationship, he saw the person in front of him as God's creation. Though sometimes his patience was tested in dealing with an awkward person, he never let that insight become obscured. Oftentimes, a charismatic man like Seán can have a particular female following. However, his sense of relationship was such that he had as many male admirers as female, and men spoke as warmly about him, and in similar terms, as the women who admired him.

As Sean had his favourite articles, he also had a favourite salutation: "I carry you in my prayer." It came from a correspondence he had with a young English woman who wrote to him in 1956 when he was editor of the Marist monthly magazine, *Our Lady's Family*. They never met but carried on a correspondence for many years, well into the 1960s. The woman's parents were French and Italian, but she had lived and was educated in England, and she moved freely among the three languages. This, of course, was a delight to Seán the polyglot and he loved the spontaneity of the flow of language. The woman had married an Australian engineer and while they were expecting their second child, they moved to Papua New Guinea because of his job. She had written initially asking for prayers for the healthy delivery of her second child – her first had been born in Australia. This second baby was going to be born far from the sophistication of a hospital maternity ward. And though there was a degree of apprehension, the woman spoke lyrically of her love for nature and the sense of being in touch with primal feelings from the earliest days of humanity. She spoke of the fact that her second baby would be born into this wild world far from the conveniences and benefits of a modern city. From the combination of her pregnancy and the jungle surroundings, she felt connected to "the whole of creation powerfully throbbing with life around her". She also felt deeply connected to "God's extraordinary love incarnate in the flesh and blood of everyday living". In conclusion to this particular letter about her sense of connectedness, she switched to French and finished with "*Je te porte dans ma prière*".

In the context of the deep personal sharing that had taken place in the letter, the context of the salutation had powerful meaning for Seán. Her words touched him deeply, with their "simplicity and directness enriched and given meaning by the context of her thinking and feeling". And after that, he used the phrase to truly connect with people who asked his prayers or those for whom he wanted to pray. It was not a case of adding names to a list, though he did that in order to remember, but it was about thinking about them and their travails, "with feeling, passionately and compassionately, and bringing them into my conversation with God". For Seán to be carried in prayer was like being held in the warmth, safety and love surrounding a baby waiting to be born, part of a loving, protected presence.

From these few insights of his three favourite articles, one might ask: was Seán the priest he was because of his Marist spirituality? Or was he the Marist he was because of the deeply spiritual priest he was? There is no discerning this, for both aspects of his priesthood were inextricably enmeshed. When one looks at Marist spirituality, one sees why he found a home within the Society of Mary and lived that charism with great integrity. For insight into this I draw deeply upon *A Certain Way: explorations of Marist spirituality* (see www.acertainway.info). Any quotations used are from that source, unless otherwise attributed.

The Society of Mary

The most fundamental motivation for the congregation of the Society of Mary was to draw inspiration from Mary the mother of God. But it was not from Mary as perfection, aloof, as the embodiment of all the great virtues, rather it was Mary always in relationship: to Jesus, to the Church and the contemporary world. This is how Seán Fagan saw *his* world – always in relationship with others; with his immediate birth family, his Marist family, his Catholic community family, his wider Christian ecumenical family, his family of the communion of saints. Seán never operated out of a dry, emotionless, propositional theology – his theology was always relational. Nothing else made sense to him in the light of his faith and his experience of God. The Marists are meant to promote a church in which the clergy do not seek a privileged role, and are meant to be among the People of God working on the basis of equality. It is stated in the Marist Constitutions "...superiors shall remember that it is Mary who is the first and perpetual superior" (MC n.178) which means, as one Marist points out, their perpetual superior is both a woman and a lay person. The early Marist fathers believed that Mary wanted to transform the Church into a place of mercy, and wanted to bring a new sensitivity and compassion into the Church. This compassion would be the mark of a Church that would be gentle with unbelievers because it saw the potential of a deeper, sounder foundation for faith. These early Marists were innovators and prophets and wanted to create something new in the Church.

The Society of Mary was founded in a world changed utterly from medieval times by the extraordinary events that were the Reformation, the Counter-Reformation, the Age of Enlightenment and the French Revolution. The Society was in the making for about 20 years before it was canonically established in September 1836. Many other religious congregations were also formed during this period to respond to demands of poverty, lack of education and lack of healthcare for large numbers of people. The new world that was evolving saw a more challenging place for the Church that previously had a central, controlling, monarchical role. There was a hostility developing towards what would have been seen as the anti-intellectualism of the Church in an age of science. Nation States were beginning to find their feet and the values of freedom and independence were guarded with great zeal. Science was on the march. Jean-Claude Colin, one of the founding fathers and eventual leader, could have led the Marists into the trenches of defensiveness, but he did not. He saw his era as a time of challenge to present the gospel in a new way. Though he was initially influenced by priests older than himself, who were quite harsh and rigorist, he was quite uncomfortable with this, and admits that:

> Since I was the youngest, I followed their decision, mistrustful of myself, although deep inside my opinion was different... Later on I recognised that, in those cases, we paid too much attention to the law and not enough to the fragility of human nature.
>
> (Cited in Kerr, *Jean-Claude Colin: Marist* p.224)

Marists now

Marists of the 21st Century are no less tasked with meeting people where they are. Their focus ought to be the "...more important and radical task of transforming the Church into a communion and a people...". To achieve this, such a Church requires a different form of leadership, not one of hierarchy so much as on the "ability to create an atmosphere in which people can recognise their gifts and have the courage to offer them for the task of the Kingdom". Seán subscribed fully to this vision of shared leadership. He excelled in the creation of the atmosphere in which people could recognise their gifts. Another of his phrases was *ex abundantia corde*. It was his encouraging phrase if a person expressed nervousness about taking on a task in theology or other aspect of Church ministry or mission, he would say "Don't worry! You will give *ex abundantia corde.*" [from the abundance of the heart].

The Church has always been part of the secular world, though for centuries it saw itself as above and apart from it. The world in which we now live has little place for organised religion in many countries. In this new culture, the gospel message must be preached again in a language that will be understood by the culture of the time. This is a culture that does not automatically grant a privileged place to Church and faith. Nor should it. The message, when allowed to grow, has its own power to convince. Oppression or compulsion never should have been allowed become part of the process. This also is echoed in Marist spirituality where there is an understanding that the Church has to begin again in this new technological civilisation and meet it on its own terms. This was the call of the founding leaders of the Society. As with all charisms, they have to be read anew in each era, with new approaches to tell an everlasting story – the boundless mercy of God.

Fr Jean-Claude Colin had a profound sensitivity to the fragility of human nature, as mentioned above. This sensitivity was to be part of the Society itself and the wider community it serves. He urged his brethren to live in the Presences that heal and mend – Jesus and Mary; to be supportive and caring of one another and to deal "sensitively, compassionately and gently, with those we serve". Mary, through her pregnancy and childbirth, gave Christ to the world. The Marist who strives to live by her spirit must be primarily concerned with continuing that work, giving Christ to the world. The Marist's role is to give flesh to the word. What the Marist historian Jean Coste (with whom Seán worked during his year of research in 1967-68) calls the 'the great NOs' refer to the stance that Marists are to take against greed, pride and power.

Seán Fagan was true to the founding tenets of his congregation. Anyone who met him in the classroom, or was blessed by his friendship, could see that his life was a witness to the spirituality espoused by the Marists. He was the merciful, compassionate face of Christ for all – without regard to status or power. As teacher, as friend, as wise counsellor, he had a particular gift for helping people towards self-understanding, but always with God as the centre. He lived his Marist charism with faithfulness, constancy, honesty and integrity. Throughout his long life and ministry he never let his Congregation down. He never shamed his confrères as fellow-Marists. One can understand, therefore, the depth of the pain he endured when for many months nobody within the Marist province would tell him the fate of the copies of his book *What Happened to Sin?*. In a letter of c. 6th April, 2012, he says to his local superior "I had to wait for over a year to be told that the books were in storage [and not destroyed]. The message I keep getting is that I cannot be trusted, I am not a normal adult. You have no idea what it feels like." And he asked, "are you doing God a favour with this storage? At what date in the future will they be burned? How far have we come from the gospel of Jesus?" Again, a week later on 13th April, he said: "I had only one request for you [at a meeting earlier that day]: to know where my books are 'stored' and how many there are. Were you afraid I would steal them or sell them? I was told that I would have to get the permission of the superior general in order to receive this information. ... It leaves me feeling that in the eyes of the SM I am a mentally defective teenager." This wound was deep and never healed.

The 'lost' books

Seán spoke of the books regularly to friends who visited him in Cherryfield. The not knowing where they were stored gnawed away in the background all the time. The effect of this was dramatically manifested on one occasion. Helen O'Grady, a close friend of Sean's was visiting him (as she regularly did) when the new local Marist leader came to visit and introduce himself. He also brought the news that one of Seán's confrères, Denis Green, had had a massive stroke. Denis was part of the CUS community in Leeson St while Seán was there. Helen, who knew Denis and another Marist who lived in CUS at the same time, Brendan Morrissey, reminisced with Seán about

Denis. When Helen was on the train back to Cork, she received a phone call from one of Seán's carers. Seán had become very agitated and upset and could not be calmed. Staff thought the news of Denis and the reminiscing with Helen had upset him and phoned her to talk to Seán, in the hopes of easing his distress. After chatting for a while, Seán calmed. It became clear to Helen very quickly that it was the issue of the books and where they were being kept that was at the root of Seán's upset. Occasionally, he became overwhelmed with the stress of it, and on this occasion the news about Denis Green was simply an overload on the persistent existing, ongoing stress about not knowing the exact location of his books.

I do not believe that this pain was deliberately inflicted; it arose from the ignorance of the depth of Seán's suffering and sense of humiliation, and from an emotional deficit than can exist in some religious communities. The concept of care and what it means for the community is an area for attention, reflection and action by orders and congregations such as the Marists. A person's emotional health does not cease to be relevant as one advances in years. This is a lesson that needs to be reflected upon, with no small degree of contrition, especially in the light of the Marist charism.

Though Seán felt wounded by some members of his Marist family, he also knew that other people were fully on his side and supported him. During his time of punishment, he received supportive letters and emails from Marists in various parts of the world whom he would have known over the years. The Association of Catholic Priests' presentation meant a great deal to him. There were also people in Ireland attempting to bring some element of justice to bear on his case. Former President Mary McAleese wrote to Pope Francis in early December 2013 and in her plea for justice pointed out that "Fr Seán ... is wounded to the core by the cruelty of the process of being silenced and he is running out of time. Would it be possible to give him some comfort that his many years

of priesthood were of worth and value in the eyes of the Church?"
Seán was by now in his 87th year.

Minimal concession

Following these representations, there was a very small concession
to Seán in deference to his age, this was the removal of the threat of
dismissal from priesthood. There was some confusion about this at
the time and it was reported in *The Irish Times* on 30th April 2014 that
all sanctions were lifted and this was carried on the Association of
Catholic Priests' website. This report caused much surprise to many
people who had no idea that any sanctions had been placed on Seán.
This was the first they knew of it. As mentioned earlier, Seán had
entrusted the fact of his punishment to a number of people, such
as the editors of the *Irish Reader in Moral Theology*, to some members of the Association of Catholic Priests leadership group and to
two journalists, whom he particularly respected, and, of course, to
close friends. Although there were a number of people aware of his
case, it was a relatively small group, and all were aware what speaking of it would mean for Seán. So everybody maintained a discreet
silence. Therefore, the report in *The Irish Times* caused a bit of a stir.
Following this, a correction of the facts given by the Irish Marists
was published on the Association of Catholic Priests' website. This
made it clear that all restrictions remained on public statements and
publishing. Therefore, only the most minimal concession was all
that was made. However, it is heartening to know that on foot of the
original, though incorrect, statement that all sanctions were lifted,
very many people sent cards and letters to Seán expressing their joy.
Exclamations such as: "The good news arrived yesterday. 'Free at
last, free at last. Dear God Almighty, free at last.' To which we add –
Alleluia, alleluia, alleluia." Others were less exuberant, but no less
sincere: "Tears of happiness that your cruel persecution has ended.
I wish you peace, joy and an awareness of how much you are loved."

Even though it was premature, given the circumstances of the very limited concession to Seán, it was a timely affirmation that so many people still felt the effect of his kind compassion and care and had not forgotten him – "speaking the truth has cost you, but you are in good company. This is what happened to Jesus and I dare say to many like him down through the centuries." These letters, cards and notes moved Seán deeply and true to form, he was anxious to reply to people. Faithful friend, Helen O'Grady typed out all the replies to the letters and cards for which they had addresses, and Seán signed them.

Seán was given the news of the limited concession from Rome by his local superior and while it was of some satisfaction to him, he was not especially impressed by it. There were some who took this lack of reaction as a sign of Seán's cognitive abilities being impaired, and that he really didn't understand the news. However, those who regularly visited Seán and spent time with him, rather than a quick perfunctory visit, had no doubt that Seán understood perfectly what he was told. He just chose not to react. He knew how minimal the concession was. While Seán certainly had some memory impairment and reduced mobility, he was not suffering from a devastating disease such as Alzheimer's. I have a letter from Seán at this time, dictated by him to Helen for typing (she had no input into the content). It was addressed to me in his own hand and signed off with his clearly-recognisable signature. In it he says: "My mobility is rather limited, but the situation here is very relaxed and I am happy enough. It was a great relief to me that the CDF changed their minds – even if only a fraction!" He knew, he understood.

Further proof of his cognitive abilities was obvious when Gabriel Daly and Seán had a long, cogent, entertaining and wide-ranging conversation when Gabriel visited him following the publication of his own book *The Church: Always in Need of Reform* published by

Dominican Publications in 2015. A book that was inspired by how Seán was treated by the CDF.

Confusion

Following the confusion about Seán's status, with claim and counter-claim, other friends of his tried to find out the exact status regarding his punishment. Mary O'Callaghan and Mary Cunningham ('The Two Marys') were friendly with Seán over several years, regularly taking him out to lunch. They were also regular and attentive visitors while Seán was in Cherryfield Nursing Home. In February 2014, Mary O'Callaghan met with Fr Timothy Radcliffe following a conference in Dublin and asked to correspond with him with regard to Seán's situation. Fr Timothy, a former Master of the Order of Preachers (Dominicans), has a significant international profile and is highly-regarded. Following the initial email from Mary O'Callaghan, he undertook some inquiries. From these initial inquiries it was his understanding that all threats to Seán had been lifted. Through further correspondence with Mary, who informed Fr Timothy that the sanctions were still in place, he undertook to contact his friend, Br Brendan Geary SM, a Marist Brother and European Provincial of the Marist Brothers at the time. Br Brendan knew Seán from his writings, but also had met him on occasion and had tremendous respect for him. Brendan also had an insight that not many others had, including many of Seán's confrères. He lived for a time in the same house as Fr Bob Nugent, who was also silenced by the Vatican along with Sr Jeannine Grammick for their pastoral work. They had worked with the LGBT community through their New Ways Ministry and were ordered to stop this apostolate by the Vatican. Brendan became good friends with Bob Nugent and appreciated better than most, the effect of the CDF's ire on a person. He generously made the time to follow up on the matter.

On foot of the contact by Fr Timothy, Brendan contacted Fr John Hannan who was still superior general at that time, inquiring about Seán's case. Fr Hannan told Brendan that threat of further sanctions has been lifted. From the email correspondence between Fr Timothy and Mary O'Callaghan that I have seen, there was a very simple misunderstanding. The "threat of further sanctions has been lifted" was understood to mean that all sanctions had been lifted. A simple mistake, but this created no small disturbance among Seán's friends who were aware of this correspondence. They were asking the question: had the CDF lifted all sanctions, while the Marists were saying this was not so and thus keeping Seán from any public comment? Or was it the case that Pope Francis had lifted all sanctions, but the CDF had not communicated this to the Marists? If this were so, then the Marists believed that the only concession was the removal of the threat to Seán with dismissal from priesthood. Given the uncertainty that prevailed and the importance of this matter I contacted Br Brendan Geary directly. He responded immediately, despite a heavy workload having just finished a General Chapter in Columbia. Brendan generously made time to meet me during a very tight visitation schedule to Ireland in January 2018. In follow-up correspondence, Brendan confirmed that what he was told by Fr John Hannan that it was a case of "no further threat of sanction" and not a case of "all sanctions were lifted".

No good end

There is no redeeming quality, no good end, to this story. Perhaps it is best summed up in Seán's own words to his Marist superior general on 22nd March, 2010. The CDF "...has the power to reduce me from a human person with a name, personality and a history, to a piece of trash of no importance, to be squashed like a fly on a window pane" (*SF Dossier/sf/JH/SF/10-07(a)*). This power needs to be halted in the name not only of natural justice, but of gospel values. When one reads many of the CDF documents, especially *Donum Veritatis* one thinks of another of Seán's phrases: "What is the doing, doing to me?" In ignoring the fundamentals of natural justice in its claims to be the sole keeper of the will of God, the members of the CDF seems perilously close to claiming the knowledge of good and evil for themselves.

Change is a necessary part of life. Without change, there cannot be transformation. And sometimes change involves death – death to the old patterns of thought and behaviour. And this is central to our Christian faith. It is what enlivens the Church – it is the movement of the Spirit, which is the active living tradition of the Church. This dynamic movement of the Spirit cannot be locked into a single formulation to describe the living tradition. The clue is in the name – it is a living tradition and can only be kept alive through "translation and interpretation so that its powerful vision can inspire each generation and every culture". (Kelly, *50 Years of Receiving Vatican II*, p.105). Theologians play a crucial part in this act of translation and interpretation. To simply repeat old formulas is to stifle growth and to damage the Church. To do so is (in the words of Matthew Arnold) simply "wandering between two worlds, one dead and the other powerless to be born". Seán Fagan understood this with every fibre of his being and worked, in his vocation as a theologian, to translate and interpret the dynamic, living tradition of the Church his whole priestly life. His life and death are a witness to his faith and a witness to the shame of those who cruelly abused him. The rather cruel irony is that Pope Francis' much heralded post-synodal Apostolic Exhortation *Amoris Laetitia*, contains most of what Seán spent all his adult life teaching, without fuss and without fanfare. But, it is notable that Pope Francis, too, has also received much criticism from a certain type of church leader for this document. But at least he did not have his voice silenced.

As Anthony Gittins tells us, disciples must not only have *felt* a presence that disturbs but to be true disciples of Jesus, they need to do more than that. They need to *become* a presence that disturbs. This is the cost of discipleship. "Every disciple is called to practice justice. That call is bound to be disturbing to some people" (*A Presence that Disturbs*, Introduction, p.xx). Seán Fagan was a presence that disturbed, but only for those whose lust for certainty has blinded them and the power-hungry who like to crush opposing voices. The CDF in its abusive exercise of power, did not break the spirit of the man – Seán was too earthed, too happy in his own skin for that, but the spirit of Seán Fagan the theologian was certainly broken – I witnessed that slow disintegration on an almost daily basis between 2008 and 2013 before he went into full-time nursing home care. And yet given the man Seán was and the witness he gave to his faith through his actions, the CDF must not have the last word. And it does not.

Who shall have the last word, then? Seán Fagan, of course – faithful priest, loyal Marist, prophetic theologian, decent human being. Not from his many excellent writings though, rather from the diary of the 11-year-old boy, who set out full of courage, hope and anticipation in December 1938 in a manner that became the pattern for his whole life:

> Seán Fagan is my name
> Mullingar is my station
> Clonmore is my dwelling place
> And Heaven, my expectation.
>
> When I am dead and in my grave
> And all my bones are rotten,
> This book will live to tell my name
> When I am quite forgotten.

(*Diary*, 16th December 1938)

SEÁN FAGAN

Select Bibliography

Making a selection of Seán Fagan's writings was not an easy job. He always wrote with the purpose to inform and educate, therefore, anything he wrote was worth reading. He said, "...since God and the things of God are at the heart of our theology, God deserves the very best that we are capable of when we speak of the divine. Language is extremely important. ... Finally, in all my efforts at communication, I have tried to speak the truth in love." (*Theology in the making*, p. 73)

In making the choice, I decided to exclude one-off articles and reflections, the exception being 'Critical dialogue: *Ad tuendam fidem*', published by *Céide*, because of the importance of the topic. I have also excluded his extensive list of book reviews written for, *inter alia*: *Philosophical Studies, Doctrine & Life, Irish Ecclesiastical Record* and *Irish Theological Quarterly*. I have, however, taken the unusual step of including his *Letters to the Editor* of various publications, because Seán always wrote those letters with an eye on educating the wider public with regard to Church matters. This care for the wider Church went to the heart of Seán's ministry and justifies their inclusion. Also, it was a *Letter to the Editor* of *The Irish Times* that brought the weight of the Vatican's ire upon Seán and made what should have been a happy retirement an experience of pain and suffering.

Books

- *Has sin changed?*
Michael Glazier, Wilmington, USA, 1977
Thomas More Book Club Selection, USA, 1978
Gill & Macmillan, Dublin, 1977; 2nd edition, 1988
Doubleday Image Books, New York, 1979
Talking Book for the Blind, NewYork, 1979

- *Does morality change?*
Gill&Macmillan, Dublin, 1997
Liturgical Press, Collegeville, MN, USA, 1997
Columba Press, Dublin, 2003

- *What happened to sin?*
Columba Press, Dublin, 2008

Collaboration in books

Coste, Fagan, & Lessard, *Antiquiores Textus Constitutionum Societatis Mariae*, Rome, 1957, 7 volumes, p. 947

Coste, Lessard & Fagan, *Origines Maristes*, vol. 2, Rome, 1961, p. 991

O'Callaghan, D., ed. *Sacraments*, Gill, Dublin, 1964, Sacramental spirituality, pp. 153-173

O'Grady, C., ed. *The Challenge to religious life*, Chapman, London, 1970. ch. 6: Formation of future religious, pp. 157-181, ch. 7: Future constitutions of religious, pp. 182-208

Flannery, A., ed. *Vatican Council II Documents*, Dominican Publications, Dublin, 1975, translation of *Optatam Totius*, pp. 707-724

von Holzen, W. & S. Fagan, eds. *Africa: the kairos of a synod*, Sedos, Rome, 1994

Flannery, A., ed. *Vatican Council II Documents: revised translation in inclusive language*, Dominican Publications, Dublin, 1996, translation of *Optatam Totius*, pp. 365-384

Mac Réamoinn, S., ed. *Crime, society and conscience*, Columba, Dublin, 1997, ch.3, To live is to change, pp. 46-66

Foster-Ryan, S. & L. Monahan, eds. *Echoes of Suicide*, Veritas, Dublin, 2001, Suicide and morality, pp. 209-215

Hanley, A. & D. Smith, eds, *Quench not the Spirit*, Columba Press, Dublin 2005, ch. 5: Spiritual Abuse, pp. 73-88

Thiessen, G. & D. Marmion, *Theology in the Making*, Veritas 2005, Theology in the making, pp. 65-73

Flannery, T., ed. *Responding to the Ryan Report*, Columba Press, Dublin 2009, ch. 1: The Abuse and our bad theology, pp. 14-24

Encyclopediae and dictionaries

The Modern Catholic Encyclopedia, Liturgical Press, Collegeville MN, USA, Gill & Macmillan, Dublin, 1994
    Original sin, pp. 620-622
    Sin and its varieties, pp. 804-808

The New Dictionary of Theology Liturgical Press, Collegeville MN, 1987
    Commandments of the Church, pp. 212-213
    Conscience, pp. 226-230
    Guilt, pp. 450-453
    Invincible ignorance, pp. 526-527

The New Dictionary of Sacramental Worship, Liturgical Press, Collegeville MN, 1990
    Experience of sin, pp. 1190-1198
    Penitential practices, pp. 941-944

Translations

Coste, J., *The Spirit of the Society* (from French), Marist Fathers, Rome, 1965. pp. 233

Coste, J., *A Certain Idea of the Society of Mary, Jean-Claude Colin* (from French), Marist Fathers, Rome, 1990. pp. 25

Coste, J., *Nazareth in the Thought of Fr. Colin, Acta SM*, Rome, 1961 (from French), pp. 299-400

Caza, L., *A Dialogue about Mary* (from French), Forum Novum, Rome, 1996, pp. 655-685

Coste, J., *A Marian Vision of the Church: Jean-Claude Colin* (from French), Marist Fathers, Rome, 1998. (with Charles Girard), pp. 477

Coste, J., *Acta SM* , 1960-1969, most of Fr. Coste's articles on Marist history, spirituality and documents

Constitutions of the Society of Mary (from Latin). Marist Fathers, Rome, 1992, pp. 155

Bradshaw, B. & D. Keogh, eds. *Christianity in Ireland: revisiting the story*, Columba Press, Dublin, 2002. A Chronology of Irish History, (from the Italian of C.M. Pelizzi), pp. 301 -334

Records and tapes

Celibacy for the kingdom, Mercier Press tape, 1968 (recorded in Vatican Radio)

Vocation is forever, Mercier Press record, 1969 (recorded in Vatican Radio)

Is Community important? Mercier Press record, 1970 (recorded in Vatican Radio)

Religious life today, 6-lecture retreat, Mercier Press tape, 1970 (recorded in Vatican Radio)

Our need of forgiveness, Mercier Press cassette, 1974

Community, vows and conscience, Mercier Press cassette, 1976

Articles

Confession and you, Catholic Truth Society pamphlet, Dublin 1967, pp. 16

The Furrow

Priestly training: new approaches, Vol.16, No. 5, May 1965, pp. 267-276

Seminary mergers, Vol.18, No.12, December 1967, pp. 700-705

The Church: liberation or entrenchment, Vol.59, No.5, May 2008, pp. 313-315

The Irish Ecclesiastical Record

Theological formation of seminarians, Vol.CV, No.5, May 1966, pp. 302-313

Perfection and grace, Vol.CVIII, No.5, November 1967, pp. 293 -302

Doctrine and Life

Our future priests, Vol.16, No.5, May 1966, pp. 227-233

Renewal of religious life: Marists prepare, Vol.18, No.4, April 1968, pp. 219-221

Spiritual direction today, Vol.19, No.5, May 1969, pp. 254-263

What's happening to priests?, Vol.19, No.7, July 1969, pp. 343-354

It is good to be here, Vol.21, No.3, March 1971, pp. 135.139

Updating confession, Vol.21, No.6, June 1971, 298-307

Divorce: a possibility for Catholics? Vol.22, No.12, December 1972, pp.625-635

Sacraments in the spiritual life, Vol.23, No.8, August 1973, pp. 404-417

Confession outdated? Vol.24, No.8, August 1974, pp. 407-417

The sacraments today, Vol.26, No.4, April 1976, pp. 264-270

No more sin? Vol.26, No.6, June 1976, pp. 375-388

Marriage in the Lord, Vol.27, No.1, January 1977, pp. 17-25

Liberation theologian in Ireland, Vol.27, No.5, May 1977, pp. 22-28

Theologians query theology, Vol.28, No.4, April 1978, pp. 246-251

Church and ministry, Vol.29, No.2, February 1979, pp. 126-131

The Church and the homosexual, Vol.30, No.8, October 1980, pp. 409-420

Theologians look at law, Vol.31, No.6, June/July 1981, pp. 390-394

Nuclear war and morality, Vol.31, No.7, August/September 1981, pp. 451-457

The laity, our sleeping giant, Vol.37, No.1 January 1987, pp. 2-11

Abortion, law and conscience, Vol.42, No.7, September 1992, pp. 455-456

Humanae Vitae in perspective, Vol.43, No.7, September 1993, pp. 426-430

Interpreting the Catechism, Vol.44, No.7, September 1994, pp. 412-417

Male and female icons of Christ, Vol.44, No.7, September 1994, pp. 440-441

Confidentiality and justice, Vol.47, No.3, March 1997, pp. 160-166

Do we still need natural law? Vol.47, No.7, September 1997, pp. 407-416

A spiritual challenge to the people of God, Vol.48, No.4, April 1998, pp. 194-205

Humanae Vitae 30 years on, Vol.49, No.1, January 1999, pp. 51-54

Is there a moral duty to pay tax? Vol.50, No.4, April 2000, pp.213-219

Facing up to spiritual abuse, Vol.51, No.3, March 2001, pp. 132-141

Going wild, or growing up? Vol.52, No.4, April 2002, pp. 194-203

From abuse to reform, Vol.53, No.2, February 2003, pp.67-77

Catholic divorce? Vol.53, No.4, April 2003, pp. 228-238

Women and men in Church and world, Vol.54, No.10, December 2004, pp. 40-45

Church renewal or Church reform, Vol.57, No.5, May/June 2007, pp. 44-51

Papal teaching, 2007, Vol.57, No.10, December pp. 40-46

Can morality be taught? Vol.58, No.8, October 2008, pp. 44-56

Supplement to Doctrine & Life

Renovationis Causam: Commentary, Vol.8, No.1, Spring 1970, pp. 30-38

New rite for religious profession, Vol.8, No.1, Spring 1970, pp. 53-56

Theology of profession in the new rite, Vol.8, No.2, Summer 1970, pp. 107-114

Perpetual superiors? Vol.10, No.6, November/December 1972, pp. 334-335

Dutch religious collaborate, Vol.11, No.1 January/February 1973, pp. 44-54

What are religious for? Ask the Holy Spirit, Vol.12, No.3, May/June 1974, pp. 9-22

Leadership and religious life today, Vol. 13, No.59, September/October 1975, pp. 27-43

Religious life and scripture, Vol. 13, No.60, November/December 1975, pp. 46-49

Celibacy for the kingdom, Vol. 19, No.82, November/December 1979, pp. 40-49

Religious Life Review (formerly Supplement to Doctrine & Life)

General chapters and renewal, Vol.20, No.93, November/December 1981, pp. 314-323

Marists and laity, Vol.26, No.125, March/April 1987, pp. 96-103

The 1987 synod on the laity, Vol.26, No.128, September/October 1987, pp. 257-265

Hope for religious life, Vol.31, No.154, May/June 1991, pp. 115-119

Religious and sex abuse cases, Vol.31, No.157, November/December 1992, pp. 316-320

The future of religious life in the U.S., Vol.32, No.158, January/February 1993, pp. 46-59

The identity of religious, Vol.32, No.159, March/April 1993, pp. 74-49

Sedos: service to missionaries, Vol.32, No.160, May/June 1993, pp. 170-172

The institutional and the charismatic, Vol.33, No. 165, March/April 1994, pp. 66-75

Preparing for the synod of bishops, Vol.33, No.168 September/October 1993, pp. 258-263

Chastity: comment on T. Radcliffe, Vol.34, No.174, September/ October 1995, pp. 266-269

Individualism and religious life, Vol.36, No.183, March/April 1997, pp. 93-100

Individualism in religious life: comment, Vol.36, No.183, March/April 1997, pp. 148-1 49

Religious living apart; comment, Vol.36, No.184, May/June 1997, pp. 138-139

Religious life in crisis; comment, Vol.36, No.184, May/June 1997, pp. 145-1 46

National assembly for the Irish Church, Vol.36, No. 187, November/ December 1997, pp. 334-335

Leadership: loss and gain, Vol.37, No.191, July/August 1998, pp. 225-233

D. O'Murchu's dubious assumption, Vol.37, No.193, November/ December 1998, pp. 161-162

Clerical religious: blessing or problem? Vol.38, No.194, January/ February 1999, pp. 23-31

Our non-inclusive Catholic Church, Vol.38, No.194, January/February 1999, pp. 37-39

Anti-poor budget in Celtic Tigerland, Vol.39, No.200, January/ February 2000, pp. 57-59

Priorities for the third millennium, Vol.39, No.201, March/April 2000, p. 100

Intimacy for celibates, Vol.40, No.206, January/February 2001, pp. 10-12

Nuns abused: questions to answer, Vol.40, No. 208, May/June 2001, pp. 146-1 56

Abused nuns: the wider context, Vol.40, No.209, July/August 2001, pp. 232-238

Survey of religious life in Ireland, Vol.40, No.211, November/ December 2001, pp. 355-361

Sex abuse scandals: will the Church survive?, Vol.41, No.214, May/ June 2002, pp. 176-1 83

What happened to charismatic renewal?, Vol.41, No.215, July/August 2002, pp. 231-233

Relativising numbers. Vol.41, No.216, September/October 2002, pp. 269-271

Religious life in a new millennium, Vol.41, No.216, September/October 2002, pp. 284-295

How can I stay in this corrupt Church?, Vol.41, no.217, November/December 2002, pp. 358-364

Is there hope for the Church?, Vol.42, No.218, January/February 2003, pp. 31-39

Homosexuals are God's holy people, Vol.42, No.220, May/June 2003, pp. 141-146

Spirituality

Sacrament of the present moment, May-June 2001, pp. 186-190

I carry you in my prayer, July-Aug 2001, pp. 230-231

The Holy Spirit is for all, May-June 2004, pp. 141-144

The Meaning of Christmas, Nov-Dec 2004, pp. 323-325

The Irish Times

Morality and abortion, 10 July 1978

More heat than light in abortion debate, 15 December 1997

The Vatican too dilatory on abuse cases, *Rite & Reason*, 9 April 2002

Voting is a serious moral responsibility, *Rite & Reason*, 22 May 2007

Reality Magazine

Morality in business, March 1998

Election 2007, May 2007

The Importance of language, October 2007

What happened to sin?, May 2008

Céide

Critical dialogue: *Ad tuendam fidem.* November, 1998

Letters

The Tablet, London
The Church and the death penalty, 25 July 1992
Wounding the Church, 17 October 1992
Marriage laws and pastoral care, 20 February 1992
The encyclical in focus (*Veritatis Splendor*), 20 November 1993
Sedos at work, 21 May 1994
Rome rule in Ireland, 12 August 1995
A walk on the edge (Rinser-Rahner), 23 September 1995
Facing the media, 4 November 1995, p. 1411
Compassion versus law, 6 July 1996
Rethinking sexual ethics, 9 May 1998
The sex abuse scandals, 14 January 2003
Reason or revelation, 13 November 2004
Benedict XVI's theology, 30 April 2005
Communion and conscience, 16 October 2005
Truth and Church authority, 18 February 2006
Limbo not a matter of faith, 28 October 2006
Aquinas in his time, 11 November 2006
Laity's instinct for truth, 16/23 December 2006
Our 'teaching' Church, 10 March 2007
Culturally conditioned teaching, 17 March 2007
Making sense of titles, 12 May 2007
No laity, no insight, 6 October 2007
Truth and authority, 2 August 2008
The origins of *Humanae vitae*, 13 September 2008
Lourdes, life and hope, 28 September 2008
Ireland's shame and future, 13 June 2009
Ambiguity of abuse, 19 December 2009
Celibacy inessential to priesthood, 9 January 2010

The Irish Times, Dublin
The President's Communion, 1-2 January 1998
Abortion and murder, 9 January 1998
The Catholic Church and women, 20 January 1998
Reception for the Cardinal, 23 May 2001
Ordination of women, 10 July 2001
Tribalism and the churches, 30 July 2001
Conscience and the Church, 18 March 2002
Catholic Church and Sex Abuse, 4 January 2003
Homosexuality and the Christian Churches, 27 August 2003
EU funding for stem-cell research, 19 November 2003
Election of Benedict XVI, 21 April 2005
World vision of Pope Benedict, 3 May 2005
Catholic Church and marriage, 17 October 2005
Catholic Church's teaching on Limbo, 6 November 2006
The Power of St. Anthony, 14 June 2007
Teaching of Jesus and radical socialism, 3 July 2007
Vatican and the Jews, 25 July 2007
Power, sex and the church, 26 November 2007
Conscience and the Church, 29 December 2007
Conscience and the Catholic Church, 16 January 2008
Conscience and the Catholic Church, 29 January 2008
Conscience and the Catholic Church, 23 February 2008
Christianity and contraception, 15 April 2008
Changing face of the Catholic Church, 10 July 2008
Christians and homosexuality, 22 August 2008

The Catholic Times (UK)
Mind boggles over substituting prayer, 12 August 2007
Follow the teachings rooted in Our Lord, 19 August 2007
When blind obedience is not enough, 23 September 2007
Our clerical Church, 21 October 2007

Is God not answering prayer for vocations?, 28 October 2007
Oath that shamed the Church, 23 December 2007
Conscience before Church, 22 February 2008
Don't ignore Vatican II teaching, 30 March 2008
'Sacred Language' just a way to communicate, 20 April 2008
A distorted teaching on married life, 11 May 2008
Shameful fundamentalists, 18 May 2008
God-given powers of reason allow us to question popes, 8 June 2008
Why a time not to embrace in marriage?, 29 June 2008
In the Father's house there are many mansions, 3 August 2008
Contraception doesn't mean an end to morals, 17 August 2008
Marriage essence in a sacred union mystery, 31 August 2008
Surfing to find the faith online, 14 September 2008
Mgr Basil puts good news into newspaper, 26 October 2008
Lessons to learn from history, 16 November 2008
Loftus is right on Church's teaching, 21 June 2009
From Maintenance to Mission in the Church, 26 July 2009
No easy solution to crisis in faith, 20 September 2009
Church same as before Council, 27 September 2009
Imperialist model of Church, 11 October 2009
Imitation of Roman Imperialist autocracy, 1 November 2009

The Catholic Herald, UK
Bishop Robinson's prophetic call for reform, 20 November 2007
Latin is not sacred, 21 December 2007
Contraception intrinsically evil?, 9 August 2008

The Irish Catholic
Latin: sacred or dead?, 20 December 2007
Congrats to Fr. Tierney, 17 January 2008
Battle over Conscience, 31 January 2008
Difficulty with plain English, 21 February 2008

Conscience and authority, 28 February 2008
Wisdom of the poet, 6 March 2008
Conscience is Sacred, 13 March 2008
New Seven Deadly Sins, 20 March 2008
Fr. Tierney is in good company, 27 November 2008

References

Barden, G. & Murphy, T., *Law and justice in community*, Oxford: OUP, 2010.

Beal, J. *et al.*, eds., *New commentary on the Code of Canon Law*, Mahwah: Paulist Press, 2000.

Chittister, J., *The Fire in these ashes: a spirituality of contemporary religious life*, Leominster: Gracewing, 1996.

Code of Canon Law, London: Collins, 2001.

Collins, P. ed., *From Inquisition to freedom: seven prominent Catholics and their struggle with the Vatican*, London: Continuum, 2001.

Congar, Y., *My journal of the Council*, Collegeville: Liturgical Press/ Michael Glazier, 2012.

Komonchak, J. *et al.*, eds., *The New Dictionary of Theology*, Dublin: Gill & Macmillan, 1990.

Doctrine & Life, ed., Bernard Treacy OP, Dublin: Dominican Publications.

Downey, M. ed., *The New Dictionary of Catholic Spirituality*, Collegeville: Liturgical Press, 1993.

Gaillardetz, R., *When the magisterium intervenes: the magisterium and theologians in the Church*, Collegeville: Liturgical Press/Michael Glazier, 2012.

Gittins, A. J., *A presence that disturbs: the call to radical discipleship*, Eugene, OR: Wipf & Stock, 2017.

Harrington, D., *What is Morality?*, Dublin: The Columba Press, 1996.

Häring, B., *My witness for the Church*, Mahwah: Paulist Press, 1992.

Häring, B., *Hope is the remedy*, Slough: St Paul Publications, 1971.

Hauerwas, S. & Pinches, C., *Christian among the virtues. Theological conversations with ancient and modern ethics*, Notre Dame: University of Notre Dame Press, 1997.

Hinze, B., *Prophetic obedience: ecclesiology for a dialogical church*, Maryknoll: Orbis Books, 2016.

Kelly, K.T., *50 years of receiving Vatican II: a personal odyssey*, Dublin: The Columba Press, 2012.

Ker, I., *John Henry Newman: a biography*, Oxford: OUP, 2009.

Kerr, D., *Jean-Claude Colin, Marist: a founder in an era of revolution and restoration: the early years 1790-1836*, Dublin: The Columba Press, 2000.

McCormick, R., SJ, *The Critical calling: reflections on moral dilemmas since Vatican II*, Washington, DC: Georgetown University Press, 1989.

Mowry LaCugna, C., *God for us: the Trinity and the Christian life*, New York: HarperCollins, 1993.

Pastor, L. von, *The History of the Popes*, St Louis: Herder, 1923.

Örsy, L. *Receiving the Council: theological and canonical insights and debates*, Collegeville: Liturgical Press/Michael Glazier, 2009.

Örsy, L. *The Art of interpretation: selected studies on the interpretation of Canon Law*, Washington, DC: Canon Law Society of America, 1982.

Rahner, K. ed., *Encyclopedia of theology: a concise sacramentum mundi*, London: Burns & Oates, 1975.

Rahner, K., *The Dynamic Element in the Church*, New York: Herder & Herder, 1964.

Religious Life Review (formerly edited by Austin Flannery OP; Tom McCarthy OP) now incorporated with *Doctrine & Life*, Dublin: Dominican Publications.

Selling, J. & Jans, J., eds., *The Splendor of accuracy: an examination of the assertions made by Veritatis Splendor*, Grand Rapids: Eerdmanns Publishing Co., 1995.

SF Dossier, letters, emails, documents supplied by Seán Fagan regarding his case with the CDF.

Vatican Documents, all documents can be access on www.vatican.va

Want to keep reading?

Columba Books has a whole range of books to inspire your
faith and spirituality.

As the leading independent publisher of religious and theological books
in Ireland, we publish across a broad range of areas including pastoral
resources, spirituality, theology, the arts and history.

All our books are available through
www.columbabooks.com
and you can find us on Twitter, Facebook and Instagram to discover
more of our fantastic range of books. You can sign up to our newletter
through the website for the latest news about events, sales and to keep up
to date with our new releases.

f   *columbabooks*

🐦   *@ColumbaBooks*

📷   *columba_books*

columba
BOOKS